Drops of
Reality

Tales from a doctor's surgery

By Dr M. A. Moss

Drops of Reality
Published by Createspace Independent Publishing Platform, 2017.

ISBN-13: 978-1544211503.
ISBN-10: 1544211503.

Editing, book and cover design: Jim Bruce
(www.ebooklover.co.uk)

Cont___

Introduction

I'M a retiring doctor, who has worked in many places and met wonderful people and had some incredible experiences. I decided to compile a few real-life stories about my work and some of the patients at my surgery, mainly for my children to read, because I've had little time as a busy doctor in the UK's National Health Service (NHS) to tell them about it all.

Apart from a few medical articles I've written for academic purposes, I also decided to write these stories for readers to enjoy. I haven't described everyday cases of sore throats, abscesses, hernia or emergency cases of people with vomiting after late-night parties with plenty of alcohol, who book an emergency appointment first thing in the morning. I've written about people who left me with strong feelings and emotions, enough to make me want to share these experiences. I have changed the names of the patients and some of the events to protect confidentiality. I'm also writing under a pseudonym.

Despite the daily unpredictability and the huge challenges and stress of my job in the NHS, I consider myself privileged to have met these people in the community. I hope readers will enjoy this colourful collection and will forgive me for any personal views about certain things.

My deepest gratitude and thanks go to the people who made this work a reality: my patients, my family and my friends.

Dr M. A. Moss, 2017

Chapter 1

Mrs Dickens in action

IT was a lovely spring day and we had just finished a meeting with the local health authority representatives. Despite the usual moans and groans from many doctors, who were not entirely happy with the increased demands being put on services and the general lack of resources available, I decided to stay positive and returned to the practice around the end of the morning session to sort out a few things.

As I went to the staff room to make a cup of tea, a familiar voice from behind me exclaimed, "What on earth was all that about?"

It seemed my colleague had finally met Mrs Dickens, a softly spoken but wily lady in her early sixties who often insisted to see me exclusively, for whatever reason, but due to my being busy at the meeting, had agreed to see my colleague instead.

Mrs Dickens was always booked (wherever possible) at the end of a session by the receptionists for one good reason – she was a very experienced story teller. Her consultations would often run up to thirty minutes (whereas the normal consultation length should be ten minutes) and she seldom gave short and sweet answers to any questions asked.

If a doctor asked her how well she was sleeping, hoping for a short, informative answer, Mrs Dickens would start by describing the night itself, then go on to say how her sleep was initially disturbed by her drunk neighbour, then elaborate further to explain that the neighbour was drunk because he was recently divorced and that, in her opinion, life had treated him rather unfairly and that although she was sympathetic, she would prefer it if he wasn't so loud.

After this she would complain about another neighbour's dog barking at the foxes during the night, then describe the foxes themselves and tell the doctor how she sometimes fed them. With her skills in non-stop talking, there was no way the doctor could interrupt her stories or try to move the conversation on to other matters.

As you can see, Mrs Dickens' extensive 'added details' were somewhat irrelevant in a medical consultation and tended to take up rather a lot of time.

I've always had a sneaking suspicion that Mrs Dickens used to wake up especially early in the morning just to be able to think up all the things she would tell the doctors about when she saw them.

My colleague complained to me that in this particular consultation, it had already taken him ten minutes just to orientate himself with the incredibly long list of medical, psychological and social issues documented in Mrs Dickens' record and that was before they even started!

Mrs Dickens assured him that although her record was long and detailed, she was only here for a 'few' things and that she'd make it 'brief'. She started by mentioning her abdominal pain caused by a small hernia. We had previously requested a surgical review and the instructions given to Mrs Dickens were to lose some weight so as to reduce the risk of the operation. She was sent to a dietician but ignored every single instruction, blaming her eating habits on her husband leaving her nine years ago for a 'younger model' (as she put it).

After her divorce she was referred to counselling to help her recovery, but unfortunately she did not follow this advice either nor did she take her medication regularly. However she was much better at maintaining her smoking habits alongside the occasional glass of wine!

I have to admit she had, after repeated nagging from the nurse and myself, agreed to cut back her smoking – from 20 to 18! She was even very proud to say that she would never finish a whole packet in one day, instead leaving one or two for the next day (which as far as I can work out still adds up to 20 a day, but Mrs Dickens did not agree!).

As for her alcohol intake, she was completely convinced that a 'drop or two' taken regularly was very good for the heart – how much this drop or two actually amounted to is anybody's guess, but I am not sure I remember reading this 'fact' in any of my studies.

She then went on to the topic of her muscle ache (as a result of Fibromyalgia – chronic muscle ache). Despite the regular supply of many types of painkillers, things were not improving for her. Unbeknown to my colleague, I had previously heard from one of our receptionists that Mrs Dickens was seen selling these painkillers in the local pub instead of taking them.

Finally, Mrs Dickens came to the topic of a physiotherapy letter, which arrived *after* the date of the appointment – an alarmingly common occurrence in our field. Unsatisfied, Mrs Dickens told my colleague that she would write a letter of complaint to the physiotherapy manager, but he politely insisted he would take on this responsibility himself. I should mention that Mrs Dickens is very fond of writing, as she used to work in a library and spent a great amount of her time both reading and writing to the local newspaper.

Feeling sorry for my colleague, I tried to be supportive by telling him about a few of my own encounters with Mrs Dickens.

One time, Mrs Dickens was vividly describing to me the pain in her knee and back. She started by complaining that she had to walk the entire distance between the Tube station and her house after visiting her friend late one evening. Reaching the pharmacy to buy some painkillers, she found it closed and was forced to continue home in the hope that she had some there. By the time she arrived it was very late and to her dismay there were no painkillers left. In a last-ditch attempt, she knocked on the door of her neighbour. Of course the neighbour wasn't pleased about this, as she had been asleep. Nevertheless, Mrs Dickens finally had her painkillers — only now they weren't working at all, and the pain was getting worse. Then suddenly Mrs Dickens woke up! The whole episode had been just a nightmare.

Unsure about why she had told me all this, and on the verge of asking her why she didn't just tell me she'd had a nightmare, I tried to explain that this nightmare may have been a side effect from the new beta blockers she had recently started taking. I then decided it would be better to simply replace them with a different type of medication.

She came back some weeks later to let me know that the new tablets were working, with no side-effects or nightmares, then quickly switched to her complaining mode.

"Do you remember when you wrote a letter in front of me to the local hospital's eye department after the optician found a little shadow in the back of my eye?" she asked.

"Yes," I replied.

"And you remember how you said you'd send it using that new system called 'choose and book'?"

"Yes..." I answered more cautiously, remembering how a colleague had recently lost a referral through this new system, and had dubbed it 'choose and lose' because of its unreliability.

"Well, they contacted me saying that the waiting time in the local hospital was very long and offered me the nearest appointment they could get. They sent me a letter, which I kept hold of and the night before my appointment I checked the address to plan my route. It turns out the hospital is about 40 miles from where I live, which is unbelievable! So I got there in time, just about, then had to wait 40 minutes because the specialist was running late. Anyway, everything was fine and then they gave me this letter."

She handed me the letter (for some reason her copy had arrived before we had even received our copy from the hospital!), but as I started reading it, I realised something wasn't quite right. The letter mentioned how Mrs Dickens had apparently worn an eye patch as a child to correct her vision and was currently wearing glasses, although neither of these facts were true.

I stopped to check the details of the letter, and found that the name was right … but the date of birth made her twenty years younger — not that Mrs Dickens minded.

Obviously the hospital had mixed up our Mrs Dickens with another.

She was furious, and I didn't blame her. I apologised, to which she replied swiftly: "It's not your fault, doc. Do you want me to write a complaint?"

I paused, then told her I'd write to the eye department directly. Despite their problems, hospitals are under a lot of pressure and perhaps an extensive letter of complaint from Mrs Dickens wouldn't have helped the situation.

*　*　*　*　*

One day, a message on my computer screen asked me to ring Mrs Dickens, who needed some personal advice and didn't want to speak to any other doctor. So I rang her at the end of my session.

"Hello, Mrs Dickens."

She answered directly, as if she had been waiting patiently all day for my phone call.

"Do you remember, doc, when we agreed that prevention is better than cure?"

"Yes…" I answered, hesitantly.

"Well, my toilet seat broke this morning and I'm pretty sure this is a health hazard. You would agree that I should do something about it, right?"

"Yes..." I again answered cautiously, unsure where the conversation was going.

"Would it be possible for the staff to ring social services for me about getting a new toilet seat?"

I suggested that our staff pass on the numbers of social services and the council to her and she could ring them herself, due to the possibility of them asking personal questions that the staff might not be able to answer.

She agreed, and a few weeks later when she saw me she insisted on telling me all about her phone call to the council – how the lady was called Mandy, she was very friendly and they had had a very long chat (of course).

But in the end Mrs Dickens didn't fit the criteria for toilet seat replacement. At this point I insisted that Mrs Dickens really shouldn't go into any more detail about the exact criteria for toilet seat replacement.

*   *   *   *   *

On another occasion, I brought up the problem of Mrs Dickens' low vitamin D levels, which she'd been aware of for some time and was taking supplements for. As if in anticipation of my question, she produced an article she'd cut from a newspaper, which claimed that in some cases it may be cheaper to send patients suffering from a vitamin D deficiency on a sunny holiday, rather than prescribing them with supplements.

"What do you think, doc?" she asked. "A sunny holiday on the NHS?"

I paused, and found I had no reply to this request. So instead I reassured her that I would bring this article up at the next local doctors' meeting, if we had time at the end. Ten minutes later, I finally sent her on her way, with a repeat prescription of vitamin D supplements, and some parting advice to spend some time in the sun where possible.

Her requests continued into the winter months. After the usual concerns about runny noses, coughs and all the rest, she added: "Do you remember the X-ray I had on my knee? You said it was early arthritis, right? And you advised me to keep it warm — you gave me a crêpe bandage too, didn't you?"

I did remember.

"Well the radiators in my central heating have been making noises and not working properly, and sometimes I feel cold. That would aggravate my arthritis, right?"

In theory, yes.

Then came the request.

"Doc, do you think I could get under-floor heating on the NHS?"

I looked at her and suggested that she contact the council to send a plumber to deal with the problem. This would probably be much faster and cheaper than sending an (already doubtful) request through the NHS. After all, it may only be something as trivial as an air lock in the system.

Happy with this advice, Mrs Dickens left and I wished her luck with her central heating — and whatever else she might face in the coming weeks.

* * * * *

Seemingly more at ease now in the knowledge that he wasn't the only one to have experienced one of Mrs Dickens' long-winded stories, my colleague returned to work, and I followed suit back to the confession room — I mean the consultation room...

Chapter 2

Sam and Louise

MY next patient was one whose name I did not recognise. A knock at the door revealed a gentleman, about 40 years old, and his partner. He negotiated himself slowly through the door — walking aid in one hand, partner on his other arm — and aimed towards the chair in front of my desk, took his coat off slowly, gave me time for a quick glance at the clock on my computer showed that three minutes of the consultation had passed already. So how could I help in the remaining seven minutes?

They were Sam and Louise, an ordinary-looking English couple. Louise explained that they used to see different doctors in the branch surgery for the past three years, and before that they were registered at a practice nearer to them in central London. That explained why I did not recognise either of them, so I introduced myself and asked about Sam's progress.

He told me about his Methadone prescription from the Drug and Alcohol Rehabilitation Centre. He hadn't suffered any side-effects, so they were planning in the future to slowly reduce his Methadone dose. Sam also mentioned that he was cutting down on alcohol, from six strong ones a day to five.

I paused. "Strong ones?"

"Yes, strong ones," he confirmed.

Reasonable progress, and I nodded, as doctors have to encourage any good behaviour.

"And how about your smoking, Sam?" I asked. Louise interjected, saying Sam was doing very well. "It's much less than before — only 10 to 15 roll-ups a day."

I suggested that he tried to cut down as best he could and he should see one of our nurses to help. Louise, however, was adamant that there was no need for the nurses, the couple could do it themselves.

I looked to Sam for confirmation, but instead noticed a yellow tint to his eyes – a sign of Jaundice. His record showed he hadn't had a blood test for about three years and when I explained the need for the test, Louise told me this was one of the things they were planning to discuss today. The phrase 'one of the things' however caused my heart to sink.

By now we had already exceeded the 10 minutes of consultation time, so I asked the receptionists to apologise to the waiting patients for the inevitable delay.

I'm aware some doctors will only deal with one problem per consultation, like sorting a blood test or writing a sick note. This is the appropriate response sometimes but in a case like this, where Sam clearly had very poor mobility and they were travelling by taxi, I decided to continue through their 'shopping list' quickly.

"So what about the blood test?" I said. Louise explained it had been requested many times by other doctors, but it had to be done in hospital because all Sam's visible veins had been damaged by his drug injection habits in the past. Their last GP had requested that the hospital sedate Sam in order to find a suitable vein, but no progress had been made yet.

They had received a letter from the Benefits Medical Assessment Agency, inviting Sam for a medical examination in a centre about 20 miles from his home, but he was unable to use public transport because he had panic attacks, and Louise said they couldn't afford a taxi to take them there and back. I said I'd do my best and write to the local hospital for an appointment for Sam regarding the blood test and send a request to the assessment agency to allow for a taxi for Sam.

Next?

"What are we doing about his weight, doc?" Louise asked. "His weight is going up and up but he doesn't eat."

I looked at Sam to clarify this statement, but was met with silence.

"Well, this is one of the reasons why a blood test has been requested. That way we can also check his glands," I explained, and made a note to refer him to an expert dietician at the hospital.

"So what about his mobility? He can't walk more than 20 or 30 yards without getting tired. And he gets terrible pain in his knees and ankles," Louise said, so I made another note to refer him to the physiotherapy team at the same hospital.

She added: "Can we ask social services to help us with shower rails? Or a wheelchair for outdoors, whichever you think is suitable, doc?"

Before I could reply, Louise seemed to remember something else from her list.

"Can we also get his repeat medications while we're here? And some cream for his dry skin on the legs?"

I started to write his repeat prescription, then reluctantly asked: "Anything else?"

"Yes, final thing!" Louise replied emphatically. It was music to my ears. "He needs a sick note because the benefits office has stopped his money."

Writing out his sick note, I asked if and where Sam had previously worked. Louise described how he had worked a long time ago in McDonald's for three weeks but didn't like it. He hadn't had a job since then. I explained that the actions of the job centre were nothing personal, and that the whole country was facing financial difficulties.

"Financial difficulties!" Evidently, Louise did not like my response. "Why are there no financial difficulties for the bankers and their bonuses? Why is there no financial difficulty when we send aid to other countries? Our NHS and education system need that money!"

Her point of view was probably better suited to a show like Question Time, not the consultation room. I was delighted to find that the sick note had printed quickly from the usually slow and temperamental printer, and I was able to avoid being dragged into such a debate.

"Here is your sick note, Sam, and good luck at the job centre. Let me walk you to the door," I offered, if only to make sure their 'shopping list' was definitely finished.

As he moved slowly from the door towards the exit, I smiled to my patients in the waiting room and repeated the apology about the delay. I very much respect the forgiving nature of people when they understand the difficulties of their fellow patients – it makes it much easier for me to carry out my duties of the day.

* * * * *

A few weeks later, I saw Louise for a brief consultation about medication for her panic attacks and depression. She was feeling down and tearful because of the stress of health and financial issues she was facing, so we agreed to increase the dose of anti-depressant tablets and she would book an appointment in the near future to give feedback on the change.

Louise paused for few seconds, then said: "I've had this rash on and off for the last four years." She showed me some of the rashes on her arms and legs, and added: "I've been using all the allergy tablets and creams the doctors and nurses gave me, but it hasn't helped. The last doctor told me it's an allergic rash and requested a test to see what I'm allergic to, which I did. Have you got the results, doc?"

I looked at the computer, where her results were displayed.

"Do you have a cat?" I asked, and she told me she did. I asked how long she'd had it, and she said about four years – same as her rash.

I smiled sympathetically and said: "You are allergic to cat fur. I'm sorry, I know it is hard. You wanted the answer to your question, and we are only here to advise — it's your decision."

She looked at me sadly, then said: "Give me the cream, doc. Lolo is my source of happiness; I talk to her when I'm feeling down, instead of waiting days to talk to a counsellor. I play with her — it gives me a sense of purpose, doc. She comes to wake me up every morning to feed her, then I make tea for Sam and myself and start the day. I can't imagine living without her." She paused for few seconds and added: "I won't let her go, thank you, doc."

* * * * *

Months passed and one day I was doing the telephone triage for home visits. I found a message on the screen regarding Sam and Louise. Sam's ankle had been swollen for a few days and he couldn't walk to the surgery. It also mentioned he was waking up with pain in his stomach, and was vomiting and feeling weak.

After my last session, I went to their home, a two-bedroom, ground-floor council flat. I entered the living room with Louise to find Sam lying on the sofa and greeted him. A younger-looking man was sitting on the recliner opposite Sam. Louise introduced me to Luke, their son, whose response was a somewhat cold 'hello, mate'.

I turned to assess Sam, who was looking fine in general: normal temperature, normal pulse and blood pressure. His abdomen was fine, and his ankle showed a good level of movement and no redness but mild swelling.

Louise told me: "He had a lot of food last night. You know, spicy pizza and a few strong beers."

"So no real emergency then," I concluded. I'd already advised him before to watch his diet and drinking habits, but I repeated the instructions anyway. "Now the vomiting has stopped, you need to cut down on alcohol, which can cause alcohol gastritis (inflammation of the stomach lining) and further vomiting."

As I was saying that, my gaze fell to his son, who had a lager in one hand and a remote control in the other. Completely indifferent, he kept watching TV.

While I organised Sam's medications, Louise said: "You know, doc, I couldn't sleep last night. I thought it would be because of Sam's bellyache, but it was because he was snoring like a pig. Doc, we haven't received the appointment for the snoring clinic yet."

I replied: "Yes, the local hospital is inundated by the pressure on the NHS. I'll ask the staff to chase it up when I get back to the clinic."

As I turned into the corridor to leave, Louise followed me and said in a hushed voice: "I need a really big favour, doc. I want you to see my son Luke."

"I just saw him," I said after a short pause.

"No, no, I need you to see him at the clinic," she explained. "He is feeling down and hasn't been himself."

I assured her I would find time to see Luke if she convinced him to make an appointment.

Two days later, I noticed Luke's name on the list for my admin appointments (for sorting out patients with more complicated issues). He arrived with Louise and I had the impression she was there to help if Luke wasn't entirely ready to start talking.

However, some time into the session he relaxed and gave permission for Louise to explain the reasons for the appointment.

"As a teenager," Louise began, "Luke was a bit sensitive, and would take things to heart. When he left school, he worked part-time in a warehouse and was going out with a lady at work. But a year later he found out she'd been dating his mate behind his back, which upset him a lot. Long story short, he applied for the army and was accepted."

Louise described how Luke used to go away for weeks on end. When he came back, he would go out with his old mates, go to Ibiza for stag parties — in short, he did everything guys at his age were doing.

"Except one day," she said. "He told us he was going to be deployed to Afghanistan. A few weeks later, we had a letter from him saying he was OK and had a lot of good friends with him. We sent him letters, parcels with little reminders of us, you know."

As Louise narrated, I noticed that Luke was miles away, probably lost in his own thoughts.

"We received a phone call from him saying he had a shrapnel injury in his leg," she continued. "He said he might stay in the field hospital for a while and that he might be coming home to recover. Later we learned that he recovered from the leg wound but stayed in the psychiatric suite, as he was suffering from severe post-traumatic stress."

Louise explained that Luke couldn't sleep, he had no appetite and was crying most of the time. He had frequent nightmares and flashbacks, and later revealed to his family that his close friend Paul, in the same division, was patrolling a remote area in Helmand Province when they came under heavy fire from Taliban fighters.

Orders were given to retreat and all Luke could remember was carrying his injured friend out of harm's way. There was blood everywhere, desperate shouting and screaming. Paul was rescued and rushed to the field hospital, then they were separated when Paul was air-lifted to a specialised centre. Luke learned the next day that Paul had passed away.

"It was a huge shock to Luke. He couldn't comprehend how one day Paul could be with him —talking, laughing, and perfectly alive — and hours later he would be dead. Not here any more, he was never going to see him again, gone forever."

Louise paused. It was clear that Luke was still suffering the effects of post-traumatic stress, and needed help.

I explained to them the options of support and gave Luke the contact information of our counselling team, and referred him to the community psychiatric team. I also wrote him a prescription for medication to help with his mental state, and gave him a card for the Help for Heroes charity organisation.

Louise was incredibly grateful and returned a few days later to share the good results of Luke's first meeting with his counsellor and the Help for Heroes team.

I said I was only doing my duty, and that the credit should go to her for bringing this to my attention before it could get any worse. Her main concern, she had said, was that Luke was slowly on a downward spiral and suffering in silence, but she didn't know how to help.

A few weeks earlier, when she was washing his clothes, a small piece of cannabis fell from one of his shirts. Louise said this brought back memories of Sam's own addictions in the past.

Years earlier, when they lived in central London, Louise had just inherited a large sum of money from her aunt – but Sam had gambled it all away. They were on the verge of eviction and it was about to destroy the family. This was why she didn't want to take any risks with Luke.

I acknowledged her concern and we both felt positive about Luke's progress. I waved her goodbye with a smile, and she gave me a cheery wave back.

* * * * *

Louise returned after a few months, as she was having frequent tummy aches. I examined her and gave her a stool and blood test to do, along with some advice about her diet.

She was waiting eagerly for me to finish, so she could tell me the news about Luke. He had managed to get a part-time job as a car mechanic in a nearby garage, where he could practise the skills he learned in the army. He had quickly gained the respect of his colleagues and last month had been invited by the garage owner to his 60th birthday party at the local social club. This was where Luke met his boss's youngest daughter, Sally, who was a volunteer at the animal charity centre in the area. Louise reported that they were very happy together.

I was pleased to hear that Sam and Louise were planning to move to an annex on her sister's farm in Kent (Louise's brother-in-law had had a heart attack and her sister could do with the company and help). Sam would also be pleased to escape from the pollution, noise and expenses of London.

"And especially from the London ambulances!"

I must have looked confused because Louise elaborated on her comment.

"Do you remember that weekend when Sam was vomiting blood? I wanted to ring 999 from the landline but Luke was ordering a pizza, so I used my mobile. The operator asked me so many questions and reassured me that the ambulance would be there soon. Do you know what happened, doc? The pizza arrived before the ambulance. I was furious! I rang them again to ask where the ambulance was, and it still didn't come until half-an-hour later."

* * * * *

Some time later, Luke came to see me and was limping, aided by his girlfriend Sally. He had twisted his ankle at work. It was very swollen and required an X-ray, some time off work and a prescription of strong painkillers.

The X-ray came back showing a small fracture, so I referred him to the fracture clinic.

Luke came regularly to see me with Sally to get him painkillers and sick notes, and they told me they had visited Sam and Louise repeatedly at the farm, and they sent their regards to our staff.

The plan for the future was for Luke and Sally to also move to the farm, where Luke would look after the cars and tractors, and Sally would tend to the animals.

I was delighted to see them so happy, and I wished them all good luck in life.

They have long since disappeared from the surgery, but the memories of them will last a long time.

Chapter 3

The Babatunde brothers

Babatunde brothers

HE was a new face to me; late 40s, moderate build, with a subdued voice and sad-looking eyes. As it was my last consultation of the day, I was not pressed for time, and my good mood meant I was open to listening to his story.

Mr Babatunde had come for a long medical report requested by his solicitor, who was trying to help him stay permanently in England. Life had taken an unpredictable turn for him, and although he would have loved to have returned to Africa to see his wife and two grown up children, he'd had a lot of bad luck and his only option was to stay here.

The topic of his home country must have brought back memories for Mr Babatunde. He told me how he grew up as part of a very respectable tribe with his younger brother, Isaac. While Mr Babatunde progressed in life to become a successful businessman, his brother used to face his troubles by hitting the whisky bottle.

Mr Babatunde decided to expand his horizons and visited the UK in search of suitable business deals. During this time he came up with a plan to raise enough money to finalise some of these deals. Communicating with traders in his country, he asked them to send him the money he needed with his brother Isaac, when he came to visit England.

He waited patiently for the day of his brother's arrival, preparing Isaac's favourite food and lining up many interesting stories about his time in England. On the day, Mr Babatunde travelled to the airport to meet his brother but unfortunately he arrived late, due to his inexperience with London's public transport system. So he missed his brother and decided to return to his flat, relying on the fact that Isaac had his mobile phone number and knew the address anyway.

Hours passed and evening came, but still there was no sign of Mr Babatunde's seemingly elusive brother. Mr Babatunde stayed awake, watching TV, in the hope of hearing a knock at the door.

Growing restless, he resorted to calling his sister in Africa to make sure Isaac had actually got on the plane and that this was definitely the day he was supposed to be arriving in England. She confirmed this and remarked that she had tried to give him some home-cooked African food to take with him. But he told her he didn't want any trouble from Customs in the UK, especially with the amount of money he was carrying.

This same scenario was repeated day after day, and Mr Babatunde found himself in a very awkward position. He couldn't call his sister to complain about Isaac's disappearing act because he knew it would only be a matter of time before word would spread around the town back in Africa, and he would be unable to return without bringing all the money to pay back what was sent (and now lost) with Isaac.

*　*　*　*　*

Many months later, Mr Babatunde returned to the surgery feeling very low and suffering from a lack of appetite, poor-quality sleep and frequent headaches. He admitted that the increased level of stress in his life was caused by Isaac's failure to show up, but he still seemed to be in disbelief of the whole situation. This manifested itself as a lack of motivation, with Mr Babatunde saying that sometimes life just didn't seem worth living.

Three weeks after the start of Mr Babatunde's treatment, he returned, as advised, to tell me things were looking up. He said he'd noticed improvements in his mood and sleeping pattern, and was delighted to tell me he had met a nice lady at the church he attended. She was a single mother with a seven-year-old daughter and, as it happened, she came from a nearby town to his in Africa. She even knew about the whole story of the disappearance of Isaac. Life seemed to be looking up for Mr Babatunde.

During a brief cough and cold consultation some two years later, Mr Babatunde was again discussing his life – updating me on his improving state of mental health and his relationship with his partner – when he returned once more to the topic of his long-lost brother Isaac.

According to a friend, Isaac had been spotted at a job centre in Birmingham, being forcibly removed from the building by security guards. He had been having a row with the staff and was apparently quite drunk.

A few weeks later, Mr Babatunde returned with his partner and their new-born baby boy for a check-up. Baby Babatunde passed his MOT – I mean his baby check – with flying colours and his parents announced that they were moving up north. Mr Babatunde's partner had had her interview last week via Skype after she applied online and sent her CV. We wished each other good luck in life and I waved goodbye, expecting they would disappear down memory lane.

* * * * *

Years passed and I had all but forgotten about the Babatunde brothers until one morning, when I was arriving at the surgery, somebody called out: "Our dear doc!" I turned and was surprised to see the familiar face of Mr Babatunde, accompanied by a young man with similar facial features.

Mr Babatunde explained that he was in the area visiting friends, and the man by his side was his son, Samuel, who had come to England to study. He gave me a wrapped present, saying it was a traditional African national costume to thank the surgery for their help in the past.

I reminded him politely that I was not supposed to take presents from patients, but as he wasn't strictly my patient any more, I would accept it and pass it on to the practice manager, who would be happy to wear it at the staff Christmas party.

After saying our goodbyes, I made my way inside and was greeted by a colleague, an African nurse, asking for a second opinion about a patient. I answered her query and I asked her (as I am interested in other nations' cultures and traditions): "What does the name 'Babatunde' mean?"

Ironically, she explained that Babatunde meant 'father has returned', in the Yoruba language of West Africa.

I smiled, remembering that neither Babatunde brother had ever returned to their homeland in Africa.

Chapter 4

Loneliness

I HAD a wonderful patient, George, whom I had known for many years. He was such a nice, friendly man, with so many fascinating stories to tell about his long life (he was now over 90 years old!).

It was always a pleasure to see him, especially at this time at the end of a session, with no other patients waiting to be seen. With time to chat, George started to reminisce about the old days (music to my ears: so much nicer than aches and pains).

He told me about his grand-daughter Suzie, who had dropped him at the surgery. She was a lovely girl, looking after him whenever she could, while managing her own young family. She had recently been to Egypt on holiday and this had triggered memories for George about his time in Egypt during the Second World War and the good friends he'd made with some of the cheeky Egyptians. It was nice to see him smile, especially after the recent tragic loss of his dear wife, his sweetheart of the past 70 years.

As if life hadn't been cruel enough, three months earlier his wife's sister had died in a horrific hit-and-run car accident; the driver had still not been brought to justice. And some months before that his 26-year-old grandson, who was in the Army, had been killed on tour in Afghanistan, leaving behind a young wife and beautiful 17-month-old daughter.

George was naturally feeling very low and struggling to cope with all this anguish, not to mention his high blood pressure and arthritis. But the real reason for his visit was a little more surprising. He explained that since his wife's death he had been struggling to manage all the post arriving at his home: endless junk mail, but with important post mixed in from the council, the tax office, pensions, insurance, the bank, savings, bills. It was never-ending and was causing him a lot of anxiety and stress. His wife had always sorted these things out, but now he had to go carefully through every piece of mail to avoid missing something important.

George was very angry and frustrated about the trouble caused by this junk mail flooding through his letterbox every day. But to top it all, since his wife's death their dog had become very anxious too, barking at every sound, especially when the postman delivered the mail. It took ages to calm the poor thing down each time.

When George took him to the vet he was horrified that one visit cost him half of his monthly pension. But the dog was his only companion and kept away the loneliness of old age. Why, he asked, could there not be an NHS for these loyal creatures? I had no answer for him.

George then told me about the frequent and irritating sales calls he was also plagued with: people pushing insurance and double glazing or asking him about car accidents he'd never had. But he had to answer all the phone calls, just in case it was his family, as they would worry if they could not reach him.

All in all, the poor man, who had lived through so much, had really had enough of life and its pressures.

I tried to deviate a little and asked him about his social activities, as he had told me previously that he used to meet up with two old friends in the local social club once a week. There they would enjoy a ham sandwich, a glass of beer and a chat. George said he was still going to the club, but one of his friends could not come any more as he was now housebound after major surgery for cancer. The other friend had gone to live with his daughter in Dorset.

I decided to mention to him some of the social functions organised at our surgery, like our group of stroke patients and their carers who meet for a cup of tea every Friday. George used to care for his beloved wife after a stroke in her later days and he nodded with a smile. I encouraged him to talk to Kate in reception to add his name.

Then I suggested that he would be most welcome to join our PPG (Patient Participation Group). This diverse group of patients would meet with our managers every 2-3 months for a light chat about how they feel about our services and how we can improve things for them.

George seemed to be happy about these ideas and I was content with the outcome.

I started typing a few notes about his consultation and suddenly the computer decided to go on strike (crashed or frozen, some people call it IT failure or computer sulk).

I wanted to ask George if he used email and had problems with junk mail there too. I could sympathise, as I also suffer from e-mail fatigue and the volume of messages landing in my mailbox every day (even every hour!). Here too, junk mail is mixed with vital messages from all over the NHS, Department of Health, Social Services, solicitors, coroners, NICE guidance, information about new or unsafe medications, treatment pathways, and all sorts. But I felt this was not appropriate and would only upset the poor man again.

In the middle of this computer dilemma I was interrupted by a phone call from a colleague in the next room, requesting help to log on to his computer, as the receptionist was having a hard time trying to assist him. He had lost all his passwords when he lost his mobile phone. The poor man had been on a boating lake at the weekend and the phone, where he stored his passwords, had slipped from his pocket into the water!

I apologised to George about the disruption and went off to sort out my colleague. On my return, I decided to spend a little more time with George, explaining that there were other sources of help and support, such as Age UK. I gave him the contact number and encouraged him to contact them for advice about any matter he needed help with.

George agreed, with his nice smile, and there was a few seconds' pause before he said emphatically:

"The knee pain is much less now with the cream you gave me last time, so I will need more of that. But you know, doc, you always make me feel much better. Have a nice day, doc, and see you again soon."

He left me with a smile and I thought about his frailty, his loneliness and his social isolation, which are such huge issues facing people in the autumn of their lives. I really wish we could do a lot or more to support people in this critical stage of their lives. Now that's something that really should be 'free on the NHS'.

www.ageuk.org.uk

Chapter 5

Mrs Folabi and the free NHS

MY last patient for the day was waiting outside. Looking at my screen the name of Mrs Folabi was all too familiar. As I called her in and then waited for her to enter the room and sit down I recalled her story.

It had been a long rambling tale about Mrs Folabi, a very imposing lady in her early thirties, and her problems with her husband. She had caught him on several occasions flirting with her sister, who was living with them. When Mrs Folabi went to work her sister would stay at home doing the housework.

But what raised her suspicion was that Mr Folabi was finding more and more excuses not to go to work as well. Now she was convinced that her sister's one-year-old baby might possibly be his and this led her to request a DNA test – on the 'free NHS'. When she was told she would need to have this done privately there was a very heated debate about why it wasn't free on the NHS.

Well, not everything is free on the poor old NHS, and I had to make that very clear. I'm still not sure she was convinced, but thankfully I didn't hear from her for a good while and I certainly wasn't going to mention it again now.

"Hello Mrs Folabi, how are you?" I said. "How can I help you?"

"Yes doctor, I have my anus completely and seriously blocked for four days!" she replied very earnestly.

"Ah, you mean constipation."

"Yes, doctor."

"OK, is there anything else?" I asked, hoping for some more information.

"Yes, yes, doctor. My shoulder is paining me for one week now."

"And how did you get that?"

"I pulled a heavy bag for a long distance to my sister's house."

"And did you take any painkillers for that?"

"Yes, doctor. I took Co-codamol from my sister, which helped."

"OK, I see," I replied, as things started to become clearer. "I think the Co-codamol may be the cause of the constipation, as it has Codeine in it, like what happened to you when the hospital gave you Codeine when you twisted your ankle last year. You remember?"

She seemed unsure, so I reminded her from her computer record how she had been walking on an uneven kerb while talking on her mobile and had tripped, twisting her ankle. She wanted to sue the council over it and as I didn't hear about the outcome I certainly decided not to ask. It was marked on her record as a drug allergy and side-effect warning that Codeine caused constipation.

"Oh, my sister didn't tell me about that!" she exclaimed.

"As a matter of interest, Mrs Folabi, is your sister a doctor or a nurse?"

"No, she's a hairdresser."

I examined Mrs Folabi, prescribed her another painkiller, which would not cause constipation, and advised her about exercises for her shoulder to do at home. I thought the consultation was coming to an end, but my sixth sense asked 'what else is she saving up for me?'

Barely had the thought popped into my head when Mrs Folabi continued.

"Do you remember my husband and me had been married for two years and we decided to have a baby?"

"Yes, Mrs Folabi, and the record shows that my colleague sent you to the hospital for that."

"Yes, he did," she rummaged in her bag and gave me the letter from the hospital clinic review. I glanced at it quickly while she was talking enthusiastically about the helpful consultant, who had explained to her the options and had asked her to continue the discussion with the GP (thank you very much, my dear colleague!).

The letter also mentioned all the options available, including IVF (In vitro fertilisation). It was also clearly written that she was not eligible for this treatment on the NHS, as her husband had a child from a previous marriage. She would need to have the IVF done privately. The consultant even added the option of going to her home country in Africa to do this as a cheaper option.

"And here I am to discuss it further with you, doctor," she said. "I had a chat with my husband and he decided if we go back to Africa to have the IVF he has to bring his children back with him to the UK. But then I will have to look after them, which I cannot do!"

"Hold on, hold on!" My head was spinning trying to keep up. "Am I missing something here? You said 'children'. I thought he had one child?"

Mrs Folabi quickly interrupted.

"Well, you know he used to travel to Africa to do business and stayed there for 3-4 months at a time. Then I hear afterwards from friends that he got married a few times and also that he had a kid or two."

Looking distressed, she added: "You see, this is another reason I don't want to go to Africa, as these wives, when they know about the IVF, they will do magic things to make it fail! But we don't have money to pay for the IVF here."

There was a pause and Mrs Folabi caught my eye and noted my scepticism. She took a deep breath and quickly continued: "I know that you signed the forms of our life insurance a few months ago for the mortgage company when we bought our house and you have seen me with my husband in his brand new Mercedes last week in the surgery car park when I waved at you. You know my husband works very hard in the charity organisation of the church and as a businessman but he sends the money to his children and his family in Africa. So that is one of the reasons I don't have money here and so I need to do IVF on the FREE NHS." She flashed me a huge smile.

I smiled back weakly and I advised her to discuss things with her husband, and maybe come back in a month or two to tell me what they had decided.

I wished her good luck and started to go through letters that needed answering. They were from patients, from hospitals, one from an insurance company and one from a solicitor asking some very strange questions to try to convince the Home Office to allow their client to stay in the UK. There was even a letter from the people next door to the clinic, complaining about fallen leaves caused from the tree in our garden blocking their drain etc .....then I could go home, finally.

Yes, surprisingly, doctors do have homes to go to! To have some rest and then to prepare for the next unpredictable working day or, as Phil Collins might sing, 'another day in paradise'.

Mrs Folabi never came back – maybe she did go back to Africa after all. Maybe it was all too much of a disappointment to find out that not everything is free on the NHS.

Chapter 6

What a beautiful mind

I HAD known Mr Roberts for years. He was a pleasant, middle-aged gentleman who had initially come across as shy but eloquent, with a well-kempt appearance and a meticulous dress sense, both casual and formal. He used to visit for the usual physical illnesses that are commonly dealt with in everyday clinic, but as I came to know him better I started paying attention to his mental health as well – he was regularly on anti-psychotic medication and appeared to be very stable.

Mr Roberts had previously revealed to me how his illness had started. During preparations for his final exams at university he had received news that his mother, to whom he was very close, had been diagnosed with terminal cancer and had only been given a few weeks to live.

This tragic news coupled with the intense stress of exams, tore Mr Roberts apart, and for the first time he felt as though he wasn't himself. It felt as though he was being told what to do by a higher being. Instructions came to him through the television or radio and were sometimes written out in books he was reading. Some of these instructions gave Mr Roberts the impression his life was not worth living. He started thinking a lot about his father's premature death from a massive heart attack and now his mother's terminal illness added to his dark mood.

Luckily Mr Roberts was able to confide these thoughts to his very understanding girlfriend, who rightly suggested he should see the GP at the university.

She went with him and they talked about how he had suffered severe symptoms of depression after the death of his dad. This was handled very well by his strong and supportive mother, as she used to talk to him on an almost daily basis (known as counselling by friends and family), and eventually Mr Roberts passed this difficult time.

The GP asked about his family history and Mr Roberts said that his grandfather had suffered from a mental illness as well. Both of these very important pieces of information were revealed at the first successful consultation with the university GP, who explained that both a family and personal history of depression or other mental health problems can make someone more vulnerable to these issues in the future.

Mr Roberts was sent to a psychiatric team, where he was admitted and treatment was started. Things improved and he continued with his life. Although he couldn't initially sit the final exam and had to have it postponed, with the help of his girlfriend and close friends he later passed with flying colours.

Life went on. Mr Roberts' girlfriend found an attractive job in London and Mr Roberts felt the time was right to apply to London universities to complete his postgraduate degree. He was also working hard at his day job as a supply teacher whilst studying part-time for his master's degree.

Over the next few months I became aware that Mr Roberts and his girlfriend had got married and life went on happily.

One day Mrs Roberts came into the surgery for a sick note and referral to the local fracture clinic. She had been skiing with her sister and friends and had a fall which fractured her wrist.

I gave her a sick note and made her referral, asking her to see me again for another sick note if needed. She also started attending regular physiotherapy.

When she returned for a renewed sick note she told me that her managers at work were not happy about the amount of sick leave she was taking. One manager had been particularly malicious in telling her about a plan in the near future to cut jobs due to the slowdown of the economy and over-spending in the department. The bad timing of this situation made her anxious, as her husband was still studying to finish his PhD in preparation for applying for a job as a lecturer.

A few weeks later Mrs Roberts came back. She sat in the chair and there was a moment of silence. I saw a tear in her eye as she began to speak and I passed her the box of tissues on my desk. Then she began to tell me how she had been made redundant. Without going into details of the unfair deal, she hinted that despite working in a government office it seemed the rules preached by such an establishment to other businesses regarding constructive dismissal were not applied by them at all. She said she had not slept for two days and so I prescribed her some light sedating, non-addictive tablets for two weeks. I asked her to come back if she needed further help.

Mrs Roberts returned many months later with an acute gynaecological problem. She said that her husband sent his regards and was very happy in his new job. His professor was a very kind man and they were working on a paper together. I couldn't hide my admiration and told Mrs Roberts to wish him good luck from me.

Time passed and I all but forgot about Mr and Mrs Roberts, until I came across a letter from the hospital in my in-tray. It informed me that poor Mr Roberts had been brought into the casualty unit by the police and had been seen by the psychiatric team on call. He had been treated and then discharged for community care observation and supervision by his GP. I decided to invite him in during my admin session due to the more relaxed atmosphere at this time of day.

He came in a week after the invitation.

"Good afternoon, Mr Roberts. Long time no see."

"Yep" he answered, with a shy smile. "I was in the hospital."

"I read the letter from the hospital but it would be nice if you could tell me yourself what happened."

Mr Roberts seemed a little embarrassed when he started to admit to his mistake. He said he had felt very well for a long time and decided to stop taking his medication. He was confident that he would now be fine without the medication and so didn't feel it was worth mentioning it to his wife, or worth booking an appointment to discuss the decision with me.

Life continued fine at first, though Mr Roberts soon fell out with one of his colleagues after an altercation over differing points of view. He also had many arguments with his poor wife over her redundancy. Adding to the usual pressures of life was a family issue regarding Mrs Roberts' sister, who had recently got divorced after finding out that her husband of nine years was cheating on her. Mr Roberts told me his wife had to drive down to Devon that weekend to see her sister, so he decided to work on one of his papers and arranged to go out with his friends for a drink later.

Due to the stresses of his work and home life, Mr Roberts had woken up very early that Saturday from a vivid dream in which there was a party at his house, with many familiar and unfamiliar people attending. He had heard two of the unfamiliar people plotting to kill someone and had woken up in a bad mood. He decided not to mention this to his wife and wished her a safe journey to Devon.

After working for most of the morning, Mr Roberts had a break and went to make a cup of tea, but upon opening the fridge he discovered the milk had run out. He quickly put on some casual clothes and sandals and set off to the corner shop down the road, leaving his house without noticing it was cold and raining outside. He walked the few yards to the corner shop, picked up some milk and went to the till, where he realised that he'd left his wallet in his formal trousers. Searching his pockets for change, Mr Roberts managed to make up all but 15p of the cost of the milk, a discrepancy that was ignored by the shop owner, Mr Kumar.

Mr Roberts returned home only to find he'd left his keys inside and had locked himself out. He peered through the letterbox and called to his wife a few times before remembering she'd left that morning.

But then he noticed something odd. He heard loud music, which was fine as he'd left it on before he had gone out, but there were strangers dancing inside his house – most probably intruders. Concerned about what he could see Mr Roberts called the police. Two policemen arrived and listened to his story, though Mr Roberts noticed one was frowning at the fact that he was wearing a short-sleeved shirt and sandals in cold and rainy weather. As the policemen looked through the letterbox Mr Roberts saw an Asian man (whom he'd never seen before) sitting on the roof of his next-door neighbour's house.

The man told him: "You are welcome to come up here and jump with me. Please don't leave me alone!"

Mr Roberts turned his face to the blue flashing lights of the police car and suddenly heard a voice telling him: "This is your chance. Run to the car and take it for a spin around London. You'll be famous, you'll be on the evening news!"

He admitted he had felt incredibly confused, but this thought process was interrupted by the harsh voice of one of the policemen saying there was nobody in his house. Mr Roberts looked at them for a few seconds and in a moment of clarity and insight told the officers he was mentally ill, had stopped his medication and asked them if it would be okay for them to take him to the nearest hospital.

Now Mr Roberts is an intelligent and knowledgeable man and has read a great deal about his illness, but it is common (and perfectly understandable) for people to think that as long as they have been mentally stable they are cured. Of course, this is not necessarily the case and as doctors we try to explain that this apparent stability is because they are taking the medication.

I have come across a number of people who loath the stigma that comes with being on medication for mental illness, and I feel that part of the reason behind this is the treatment of mental health as a taboo in our society. Many people simply don't realise that it can affect anybody at any stage of their unpredictable life. Mental illness is really surrounding us: in the street, at work, between friends and family. It has affected many famous people: the pioneer of mental illness research Sigmund Freud; great leaders like Abraham Lincoln, Winston Churchill, Queen Victoria and George Washington; great artists such as Pablo Picasso; great actors like Jane Fonda and Sir Anthony Hopkins and great scientists such as Charles Darwin and Albert Einstein.

Mr Roberts took his medication as advised and left with the same shy smile he came in with, leaving me with a few seconds to contemplate the stigma of mental illness and the recent government announcement that there would be cuts to mental health services, when in fact the opposite was needed.

Despite the fact that we convey this point of view to the decision makers in many repeated meetings, we sometimes feel as though we are banging our heads against a brick wall. Hopefully someone will listen one day and understand our concerns.

Chapter 7

The football team and the coincidence

IT was a nice, easy-going afternoon session, steadily working through the list of visitors (I sometimes think of patients like that, as some really do just come for a chat!).

The last one was Miss Williams. She was in her late thirties and quite fit and healthy, according to her record. But a note on the screen with her record made me frown. Another doctor had requested she always be booked for a double appointment, especially if she was bringing one of her children along.

Oh, now I remembered Miss Williams. This was the lady who believed in the 'two for the price of one' culture – deciding that as long as she had an appointment then the doctor could always see her children at the same time!

Now, despite the limited consultation time of 10 minutes, occasionally we can stretch to one minor additional request, but in this lady's case it was never minor and more often multiple.

She was blessed with many children from two previous partners. I had met her first partner on multiple occasions and Miss Williams had regularly tried to convince him to stop drinking, and provided all kinds of incentives to encourage him to get a job.

But he was very resistant to both ideas and she would tell me how he would blackmail her into giving him money for booze so he would be in a good mood to treat her nicely and play with the kids. Without his drink he was not a very nice person at all, to her or the children, but the drink was also

42

the main cause of their poor relationship. They argued almost every day, and eventually she asked him to leave.

A few months later Miss Williams dated a friend of her first partner, and they lived together for a few years. She described him to me one day as a hard-working scaffolder, earning good money. But she also hinted he was a bit introvert and didn't talk much, especially about his feelings.

Then one day she told me that sometime ago, over a weekend, she had woken up and couldn't find him in the house. Then she discovered he had taken his clothes and belongings. She found a note in the kitchen saying he couldn't explain himself but he didn't want to know or see her and the children any more. With that he simply disappeared from their lives.

It was very difficult for her in the beginning, but with the help of her supportive mother and friends, Miss Williams pulled through that difficult patch of life and later came across her current husband. She used to joke about him that all he was good at was making babies.

However, one day she was booked for a six-week postnatal check, which went routinely well until I broached the question of contraception. This was quite usual, as some ladies don't seem to be aware that another pregnancy can happen even with breast feeding (although it is less common).

She laughed and firmly declined to even discuss it. I remembered then from previous consultations that she didn't believe in contraception and now had a total of 11 children. To add to this, she hinted that she might think of adding another one! So she had a full football team – and one on the reserves bench, too.

I have to admit, after she left, I wondered at the heavy responsibility of such a big family, both financially, physically and psychologically, especially as I had heard that her husband was not working due to chronic recurrent back pain.

This prevented him from being able to do the heavy lifting his usual work as a labourer in the building industry required.

Miss Williams used to come with her mother occasionally and mentioned at the time that the mother was very supportive and helped her in looking after the kids.

Now having many children can be considered a personal choice, a human right, a matter of tradition or religious belief, and something not for others to interfere in.

Much later that afternoon, while ploughing through my post and emails over a rushed cup of tea, to make sure there were no urgent matters that needed sorting out before finally heading home, I came across an e-mail forwarded by a colleague.

It included a copy of a point of view expressed by a consultant at a reputable London hospital. It was part of a long letter of frustration this consultant had sent to a national newspaper, and it made me laugh (in irony) at the end of a long and weary week.

I have added below a summary of part of the content – and will let you, my dear reader, make your own conclusions.

.... *A lady in her mid-thirties visited the senior consultant at his hospital, where he had treated her on many occasions. During one such visit he had a little time to spare, as several other patients had not turned up. The lady started chatting and she mentioned that her mum was so proud of her and called her "the breadwinner of the family".*

The consultant was curious to know why (as he was sure her notes said she was unemployed) and asked her to explain.

The story went like this: Some time ago her mother rang the Department of Work and Pensions (DWP) to report that her daughter was ill and couldn't look after her children properly. The DWP agreed that the children would need to be fostered. So her mother volunteered to be the foster parent for the children and duly received about £700 per month for each child. This considerable tax-free income meant that nobody needed to go to work. As that income would be increased if there was no fathers around, he was duly asked to leave.

The consultant added that on top of this, additional benefits like free housing, free council tax, free dental, free schooling, free prescription and many other benefits were also available.

Roughly calculated, the consultant acknowledged that all the above tax-free annual income and the benefits would be roughly equal to his own income after years of very hard study, many books to read, endless lectures and examinations, sleepless nights during training, and a very hard working career to reach to the position of senior consultant in a reputable teaching hospital in the capital.

You can imagine his despair when the lady concluded that every baby made money, and there was no need for anybody to go out to work.

His final sentence was to advise us to please keep working hard to pay our taxes, as there are many 'breadwinners' in our financially struggling country that are dependent on our taxes.

Chapter 8

A labour of love

I HAD known Mrs Anderson for many years as a pleasant, very hard-working lady in her mid-60s, who had been very loyal to her beloved late husband, who had sadly lost his life a few years earlier after a long battle with a merciless cancer. She had taken some time off work to care for him as his illness worsened.

Time passed and she recovered from the sadness of her loss. When she returned to the surgery again after a while, she was with her godson, Jordan, who had just registered with our surgery. Mrs Anderson introduced him to me as her cousin's son, who had come to England to study business at university. She said she would be looking after him.

Jordan was a bright-looking youth dressed in sport-casual clothes. He looked slightly shy, encouraged from time to time by his godmother, who seemed very proud and happy about his steps in starting university.

She added that she used to support him when he was a little boy at school in the Caribbean, when she used to visit every year to enjoy a break from the stressful life of London and to enjoy the sun and time with her extended family.

The days went by and Mrs Anderson sometimes came in with a few health issues and always used to report back on Jordan's progress at university.

Jordan had a group of friends, who used to visit him at her house. I noticed her concern about some of them as she mentioned a few sentences about smoking weed, drinking and the fashionable use of 'legal high thingies', as she called them.

She had discovered these incidentally one day when she told Jordan she was not feeling well and would go to sleep. While she was in her room reading, she overheard Jordan and one of his friends discussing the best place to buy weed.

I smiled when she added that she had a stiff word with him a few days later to keep the boundaries, and she reminded him of the rules of the house – no late nights and no bad influences from friends.

She explained that she had spent all her time, and a good deal of her savings, hoping that one day he would be a good citizen and he would repay her. She was very much looking forward to his graduation day.

I smiled and nodded in approval. Of course, I had to respect the confidentiality of her godson's medical record and did not reveal any of the information regarding his smoking or drinking habits, which he had told me about in his own consultation the previous month.

Time flew and Mrs Anderson was back again, telling me how happy she was that Jordan was now in his final year at university. With a cheeky grin she hinted that he had told her about a nice girl he had met through a mutual friend. She came to study marketing and after finishing study started working for a company in the City.

The girl planned to return to Canada, where her Caribbean parents were now living. Mrs Anderson added that the nice girl had come round for tea once and was introduced to her.

A few months later, Mrs Anderson came in for an asthma check, as her asthma had been exacerbated by a viral infection. She looked a little tired, a little uncomfortable and not her usual self.

I asked her if her cough woke her up at night. She said it did sometimes, but that she did not sleep very well nowadays anyway. She paused for a second, followed by a short sigh.

Then she added: "Jordan is changing a bit. I feel that he is for some reason trying to cut me off from the rest of the family, especially from the people I used to help financially — and still do if I can. I don't know. I have a feeling this is the influence of his girlfriend. I think she's controlling him."

Three months later, Mrs Anderson came in for a blood pressure check, to get a repeat prescription and for a consultation over new symptoms of occasional headaches. With a big smile, she announced that Jordan had passed his final exams and she had attended his graduation in an atmosphere of joy and happiness.

Then she mentioned she was getting the occasional headache in the morning and sometimes in the evening. I checked her blood pressure, then smiled at her and asked if she was taking her medication regularly.

She replied emphatically: "Yes."

I followed that by another question: "Do you sleep well?"

For a brief moment I noticed her complexion changed a bit and she asked: "Why?"

"Because your blood pressure is a bit high, and that is probably the cause of the headaches."

She then told me, Jordan has been applying for jobs and I was very happy when he told me he got two offers. One was in a City firm and one was in Canada, which pays more than the City firm. He said he might think about going to Canada — it's where the girl wants to go to be with her family."

This made Mrs Anderson a bit anxious and possibly reminded her of the loss of her husband. That was probably the main cause of her poor sleep.

I gave her some light sedation tablets to help her sleep, sent her for some blood tests and told her to come back for a blood pressure re-check in two weeks.

Mrs Anderson returned, with a better night's sleep, and told me that Jordan had accepted the job offer in Canada and was going at the end of the month.

She added: "I know that I'm going to miss him very much, but I know this is the rule of life. At least he promised to keep in touch, and I really wish him all the best."

A few months later, Mrs Anderson came to have a short insurance form filled in. She mentioned that Jordan was doing well in Canada. He had visited his girlfriend's family, and he regularly kept in touch with her.

Mrs Anderson and her family were planning for a family reunion in the Caribbean in a few months and she also told me of the good news that her family had found her a piece of land for her retirement near the sea, as she had requested. She said she was going to buy it and had sent the deposit over already.

Mrs Anderson then revealed, for some reason, that the piece of land had exhausted all her savings and she was counting on her godson paying her back in small monthly instalments, so she could start building her dream retirement bungalow.

After a while she booked an emergency appointment with me, as she had got a nasty insect bite around her ankle while gardening. She also told me that Jordan and his girlfriend were planning to marry and had bought a house together.

He had called her recently to say he would not be able to attend the family reunion as the living expenses and the mortgage on his new house meant he couldn't afford the travel costs.

Mrs Anderson attended the family reunion and came to see me with a respiratory viral infection caught after the long flight home. She told me with a sad voice it was a nice reunion and she enjoyed seeing the good people she grew up with in the Caribbean. But she was a little surprised to hear from her cousin (Jordan's mother) that Jordan was barely calling her any more. She also found out from another relative (who went to school with Jordan) that he had seen Jordan's wedding photos on Facebook.

She decided that when she was back in England she would ring him to see what was happening, as he had not contacted her since he had announced his decision to marry.

Mrs Anderson told me she had called him to ask about the wedding and he had replied, in an emotionless tone, that he was planning to tell her but it came around too quickly. He said the celebration was limited, with only the girlfriend's family and his friends from work attending. He then added that due to financial pressures he would probably be unable to repay her the money she had spent on him for his education in the UK.

Mrs Anderson was so shocked, all she could do was wish him good luck and hang up the phone.

I was lost for words, so I just told her she needed to look after herself.

* * * * *

One morning, as I was rushing to the car for a home visit I bumped into Mrs Anderson. I had been concerned about her lately, as she was having a hard time and had lost a lot of weight.

Her sad face said it all when she approached me quietly and said: "I need to see you next week, doc."

I smiled at her and replied: "Yes, by all means. You can book double appointment at the end of a session if we need to cover a lot of ground."

A few days later she came to see me to discuss her options on casual terms, seeking advice from an old man like me.

Her wish was to retire to her home country in the Caribbean and I respected this. Should she reside in a nursing home there, or should she sell the land she had waited all her life to live on to pay for a private nurse or carer to look after her here in England, (as her osteoarthritis of the knees and shoulders was worsening)?

She left a packet of chocolate and a card for me at reception —and disappeared from the radar.

Checking the post one day after a busy morning near Christmas time, I found an attractive envelope. I opened it to find a nice Christmas card from her, signed 'an old friend', from her sheltered retirement accommodation in the Caribbean, with a nice view of the sea.

There was a little note to say she was content and added that her godson was very busy now, with his new arrival of a little baby boy.

Unfortunately, not everything had turned out so well for him, as his wife had had a horrific road accident during the icy conditions that had hit Canada. She suffered severe facial injuries and few broken bones, as she had been trapped in the wreckage of the car.

That was the last I heard from her.

But I have always thought how inspiring a godmother's love can be. Despite her own loss, this wonderful lady gave her time, love and savings to bring up this young man and set him on the road to success.

In return, she was happy just to know he had made it and had found his own happiness.

I think in the end it would not really have mattered to her where she retired, as long as she knew her job had been well done.

I'm so glad it worked out for both of them in the end.

Chapter 9

Who needs crosswords?

I HAVE met many people with a very sharp memory for names, and a few opposites – as some names are difficult to pronounce and remember. In some countries or languages, names mean something specific to the people, while in another nation or language, it's just a name.

Nigeria is such a country, where a name can tell you a lot about the person, and I have always been interested to know these meanings. For example, a name like Babatunde in the Yoruba language means 'father returns' or 'a father has returned'. This generally refers to a male ancestor who is deceased, declaring the bearer of the name as being the same in character or appearance as his deceased relative.

Some other examples of interesting names with meanings I have come across are:

OLUWASEYIFUNMI, which means 'God has done this for me'.

ORITSEMITSERUDEDE (God gives this last).

MOYOSOREOLUWA (Thanks to God for the gift).

CHUKWUNONYELUM (God is with me).

KAOBICHUKWURAH (God's big heart).

This can also be seen in British surnames in the past too – names like Wheeler, Cooper and Butcher referring to a trade, or Johnson and Richardson referring back to a father's name.

If you don't know the language it can seem like a long string of letters. Imagine trying to accurately pronounce such an unfamiliar name when calling the person for their consultation when the digital call board is not working.

Our reception staff have become very good now through experience, but with many variations it can still be hard to remember. Thankfully some of our patients take pity and allow us to abbreviate their names to Olu, Ori, Moyo or Chuk (much as Thomas can be Tom and Katherine becomes Kate).

Years ago (when I was much younger and less busy-minded!), I used to have a very good memory for names and faces and I had no problems with crosswords either (when time and circumstances allowed). But with increasing responsibilities and stress, I think I have started noticing a weakening of this skill.

One day this was certainly proven when I called in my next patient, a lovely lady in her late 80s.

Not checking the record on my screen, as I usually do, I smiled and said: "Good morning, good lady, long time no see!"

She smiled back but seemed a little confused.

"But doctor," she answered, "you just saw me last month, when you asked for a scan, increased my medications and said come back to check my blood pressure. So here I am to check the results of the scan and blood pressure, as you said!"

There was a brief awkward silence in the room. Embarrassed, I stared at the computer screen and she was absolutely right.

Had I remembered any of this? The honest answer was no, and what made the matter worse was the alert flag in the corner of the screen saying the patient was eligible for dementia screening.

I paused for a second, with an ironic smile, thinking that this lovely lady was far more on the ball than I was! Maybe she should have been asking me questions like 'what is your address?' or 'what is the date today?'

I quickly checked her scan results, took her blood pressure and reassured her, hoping my error would be forgotten. However, it taught me not to take things for granted any more.

I remember we used to have two very good nurses working with us, who were a great support to both doctors and patients. One day the senior nurse mentioned that she sometimes had problems putting names to faces, but I didn't pay a lot of attention to it, as long as she could remember her own name and those of our team.

This nurse would often come to me to report on a recent case or to discuss a home visit. She would usually start by describing the patient to me.

"I visited that lovely man, who is a bit tall with grey hair, wears glasses, lives alone, and loves his golf and fishing. You remember his wife died after the struggle with terminal breast cancer? You know him, don't you? You helped him a lot to get all the support they needed during his wife's illness....."

Because of the pressure of work and time, wracking my brains to put a face to this description from several thousand registered patients on my ever-expanding list, I would try to focus on the problem and how to solve it.

Sometimes though, if I was lucky enough to have a moment in the staff room for a quick cup of tea, I would consider this as a mind-challenging exercise (a better alternative to the usual crossword puzzle).

This might appear to some people as a bit disrespectful, but for me it was a positive bit of mind exercise, where sometimes I could score as high as 8 or 9 out of 10! Not bad for a busy old doctor trying to keep in mind all the diseases, drugs and side-effects alongside the names and conditions of over 6,000 patients. Add to that the ever changing software and technology, with dozens of varying passwords and pin numbers that need regular changing, I think we all live in a very mentally challenging world!

One day Dr Newman, one of our senior GPs, was in the staff room just as I was finishing my tea. Often we can work a whole day in the same building and not see each other at all, so it was nice for a moment to catch up between sessions. Like my senior nurse, Dr Newman liked to quiz me about my patients and she too had a weakness with names.

So the game began.

"You know that short, stout patient, that Afro-Caribbean gentleman who wears the glasses, who brought chocolate for the reception staff last Christmas?"

Sometimes this could lead her into some rather embarrassing situations. One day we were at a regional meeting together when she saw what I supposed to be an old friend or acquaintance of hers. They kissed and hugged each other, asking how each had been, and how long it had been since they had last met.

However, after the lady had left, Dr Newman turned to me and asked who this lady was! I was very surprised and could only vaguely remember perhaps seeing her at another meeting. I had to admit to Dr Newman that I really had no idea and was actually going to ask her the same question.

This is, however, not just a condition limited to doctors and nurses. Strangely enough, I have also spotted a handful of our patients doing the exact same thing to me.

"You know, doc, those little pink tablets, the painkillers you prescribed me two years ago. I got them from that pharmacy across the road. You know them, don't you?"

This patient will then be surprised when you don't answer, as doctors are supposed to know all the medications they have ever prescribed by sight.

The fun can even extend to the names of medical conditions. So your poor stressed brain not only needs to work out who you are talking about and what the medication is, but also the mystery disease being described or mispronounced. Add the odd heavy accent and you could soon end up in deep water.

I once had a very talented French locum doctor work for me. Her enthusiasm and hard work, coupled with the many humorous conversations we had, were really unforgettable.

In addition to the usual problem with names, she possessed a great skill of describing her patients to a tee with her lovely French accent.

With her, 'think' became 'sink', and 'thank' became 'sank'. The issue of confusing 'ear' and 'here' could lead to some very funny conversations, and I confess that sometimes I did tease her with some deliberate misunderstanding.

There was also the matter of word order – as some of the continental languages swap certain words around. One example was when we were discussing a patient with an inflammation of the 'here' (sorry, ear). She repeatedly mentioned a condition which she described in her French accent as 'mediaotitis'. Again I wracked my brains to work out what this mystery condition might be, concentrating hard to disentangle it from the rest of the conversation peppered with many 'sinks' and 'ears'. Finally the penny dropped.

"Otitis media! (inflammation of the middle ear)" I exclaimed in triumph

She looked at me blankly "Yes, that is what I said, mediaotitis of the ear!"

But my favourite had to be the day she came to tell me about her patient with a swollen foot. Having negotiated our way through to identifying the patient's name, she rapidly started to tell me about his condition.

I thought I might have misheard when the word 'goat' came up repeatedly. Discussing the best treatment she continued mentioning this goat. I concentrated hard, desperate to understand where this goat had come in. But as she discussed the various medications, the matter grew into a full-blown goat attack.

I could hold back no longer and asked her: "Where did this goat attack the patient? Did it attack his foot?"

She looked at me as if I had gone mad – then grabbed a pad off my desk and wrote a word very firmly and handed it to me.

"Oh, I see…" I couldn't help smiling; the word on the paper was 'gout', the cause of the swelling in the foot!

I suppose such little misunderstandings could explain why the French have often considered the English a slightly eccentric race, to say the least.

Chapter 10

Life can be so cruel

IT had been a relatively reasonable day and I was approaching the end of the evening session. My next patient was Mr Collins, a quiet man in his early 40s, who I recall often came accompanied by his supportive mother. She was a very well-spoken lady, who paid great attention to her appearance, always coming with delicately painted nails and light but effective make-up. I became aware early on that she was a retired nurse and well understood her son's condition of severe and recurrent depression with suicidal intentions and deliberate self-harm, which he'd had since he was a teenager.

"How are you keeping, Mr Collins?" I asked him.

He told me about his somewhat reasonable mood but said he had difficulty getting to sleep at night. As we had discussed this point before, he mentioned that he had been wise enough to avoid the addictive sleeping tablets and had applied the advice given for improving the quality of his sleep. His mother had helped by giving him a tablet or two of an over-the-counter herbal medicine.

Mr Collins also said he was learning more about the computer and improving his skills, again motivated by his mother.

"And how about your physical activity?" I asked.

"I go to the gym sometimes and walk the dog when I can. Oh, and every week I go and see the kids, too."

I remembered he was divorced and had two kids. Mr Collins' marriage had broken down during a severe episode of depression. His poor wife at the time couldn't understand the calamity of the problem, shouting at him to pull himself together. She couldn't comprehend that he lacked motivation and had lost interest in doing anything he used to enjoy, either in his married life or during his work as a landscape gardener.

I had wished at the time that the whole nation (and mainly the people in power) would try to understand and provide more support for mental illness, or at least avoid cutting the budget.

Mr Collins was taking his medication regularly, with no side-effects and certainly no suicidal thoughts. As I praised the support his mother was giving him, I heard her faintly saying that she wasn't doing so any more, and with a weak voice explained that his sister would be taking on the responsibility.

For a second I thought she had given up on him, but as I looked at her for some clarification, I noticed a deep sadness in her.

She paused for few seconds and said: "I have a terminal illness and probably won't last till the next review of my son, as you like to see him every three months to keep an eye on him."

"Terminal illness?" I said.

"Yes, advanced cancer with no cure and only palliative care for the next few weeks."

I froze in my chair. Despite years of hearing shocking news of differing degrees, this one was heavy, as if a death sentence had been issued in court to someone who was very dear to my patient (and whoever is very dear to my patient is in turn very dear to me).

I gave Mr Collins a sick note of three months and said in a hesitant voice: "Good luck and goodbye."

I took a break for a few minutes to reflect and comprehend what had happened in the consultation. I wished it was a dream or a nightmare but it wasn't, it was the harsh reality of life. You see somebody, a few weeks later they have fatal news and then after a few more weeks they are but a memory.

This situation reminded me of one many years ago, when a gentleman in his late-50s, with an impressive physique, came to the surgery with his wife. While having a chat with Dr Newman about his wife's more frequent visits lately, the man proudly stated he had never had a check-up and was very healthy and didn't need to see a doctor. Dr Newman advised that he should come in for a health check anyway, since he didn't have one on his record.

A couple of weeks later, he came to me to have a general check-up as requested by Dr Newman and his wife, but still insisted he needed 'absolutely nothing else'. I updated his record accordingly to say he was a non-smoker and only drank alcohol occasionally. I explained the need for a health check for people around the age of 40-50 as some illnesses may start appearing.

I checked the gentleman, who was in really good health – with normal blood pressure, good heart, normal chest and abdomen – and I requested routine blood tests.

The next day, when I was reviewing his results, I frowned at the extremely out-of-range nature of his liver functions, with very high enzymes. I rang him on his mobile to say I needed to see him to explain some of the results.

He came in two days later and I asked him about any possible symptoms he might have been experiencing. He said he'd been having the odd indigestion and some abdominal discomfort recently but nothing that really bothered him. I explained the need to find the cause of the high liver enzymes and told him I had already requested an urgent scan on his liver and that he would receive an appointment, which he had to attend.

Following the appointment of his scan, I was surprised to read a fax from the radiology department telling me the man had a sizeable liver tumour. I contacted him, requesting to see him with his wife to explain the difficult issue and the urgent referral to the specialist centre to deal with this problem.

He came in two weeks later to tell me he was starting chemotherapy soon and couldn't go back to the physically demanding work he was doing before. I supported him during his difficult terminal time of about three months, which passed very quickly.

I remember another example of a call from our experienced nurse for a second opinion about one of our nice patients, a man aged 70-plus, who had sadly been given the diagnosis of cancer a few months earlier and had been given chemotherapy, with some undesirable side effects.

During a follow-up at our surgery, he revealed to the nurse that his main problem was that he had not been able to sleep for a week. I thought this was down to his illness or the side-effects of his medication, but as I paused to think for a second he explained the real reason.

"About a month ago my only son, 38 years old, fit, healthy and a sports fanatic, developed thigh pain 2-3 hours after he had been playing football. He ignored it at first, assuming it was down to him bumping into another player, but when the pain got worse he went to his GP. The GP sent him for blood tests and for an X-ray, where a suspicious lump in the bone was discovered. So he was referred to a specialist and it turned out it was a very aggressive type of cancer. Despite many investigations and chemotherapy he unfortunately succumbed in my arms a week ago."

The nurse hugged him and I expressed my sympathy for his great loss.

I prescribed him sleeping tablets and reassured him, offering him all the support he needed and informing him of the open-door policy to see me any time.

As I went back to my room, I could feel my steps getting heavier and the distance to my room getting a little longer.

Weighed down by the sympathy I had for the sadness of human beings, especially the ones we know well. Sadly, four months later this gentle soul also passed away.

I kept thinking about how cancer is such a frightening and merciless disease. There are hundreds of types of Cancer. Many are controllable and treatable if caught early enough, but some are uncontrollable and incurable, despite the huge advances in science. Still, I have the feeling that more resources can and should be directed into research fields, instead of wasting money on wars, or chasing a mirage called 'weapons of mass destruction'.

For advice about the topics mentioned in this chapter please visit the web pages below for cancer support:

Macmillan cancer support – www.macmillan.org.uk
Cancer Research UK – www.cancerresearchuk.org

Chapter 11

The power of positive thinking

I MET Lila, who was in her early 20s, when she became my patient after one of our senior partners sadly passed away. I was therefore already aware of the unlucky events of her childhood.

Lila had been in an accident which had left both her legs paralysed. However, she was only paralysed in the physical sense of the word, compensating with a brilliant mind instead. You could see the determination in her eyes when she spoke about something she wanted to achieve, and I witnessed this when she decided to learn to swim. Then again when she wanted to go to university to take a degree in business, whilst also struggling to cope with the knowledge of her grandmother's recent diagnosis of recurrent breast cancer. Despite everything, she eventually decided to also do her Masters degree in business − and passed with flying colours.

At the end of one of my consultations with Lila, I was asked to go to a home visit. Since she was on her way out, I walked with Lila to the car park and noticed how successfully she negotiated every obstacle with her wheelchair. When we reached the car park I noticed she had parked in an ordinary space as opposed to the disabled one, which was occupied. When I offered to help her to get into her car, she smiled, declining the offer, saying: "Save your energy for the other patients, doctor."

She managed to shuffle her body into the adapted disability car and pull the folded wheelchair into the space designed for it. I was totally impressed as I went to my car to attend the home visit.

To my surprise, I found that the home visit was for a young lady with back pain, who reported she could not leave her bed. When the nurse asked her who would open the door for the doctor, as she was apparently bedbound, she answered that she would!

The next time I saw Lila she was smart enough to book the last appointment, as she knew I would then possibly have some time for a talk or a joke, depending on the mood of the day.

During the consultation, she requested some help to lose some weight in preparation for the happy event of the wedding of her older sister, Rebecca.

Lila's sister had not made the same steps in life as her physically less able but very positive sibling. Instead she had decided not to continue her education after leaving school, working instead in a local corner shop as a sales assistant. She was now about to marry her long-term partner, with whom she'd had an unsteady and volatile relationship for many years, caused by his addiction to alcohol and drugs. I am not one to judge, but I couldn't help but notice the contrast in the two sisters' circumstances.

Thinking of Lila brings back many memories of events that made me think. I remember when she pointed out to me politely one day that the hospital had sent her a copy of some letters which were still being addressed to her previous (deceased) GP. I explained that we had reported this error to the hospital many times over the years, writing to them repeatedly and to different departments. Sadly, this had also happened with patients receiving reminders and appointments when they had passed away. The slowness of the administrative wheels in these big institutions seems to make them completely blind or indifferent to the offence they cause. Sadly even death does not seem to end the relentless work of a GP.

On another occasion the hospital wrote Lila a sharp letter telling her she had not attended her outpatient appointment, so she had been discharged from the hospital and would need to go back to her GP for another referral. She was confused and upset as she had in fact not received any such appointment. Then a week later, (and two weeks after the alleged appointment that she had not attended), another letter from the hospital landed on her doormat. It was the invitation to attend that very appointment.

What could I say? I smiled, made the usual and frequent apology for the overburdened and disconnected NHS system. I then made a new hospital referral for her, putting her back once more on the NHS hamster-wheel to wait for another appointment.

I really admired her endeavours when Lila mentioned she had found herself with a few hours free each week and had decided to volunteer to help some disabled people at a local charitable organisation.

She talked with great passion about the good work this charity was doing and she mentioned shyly that this was also where she had met her handsome new boyfriend. She said they had got to know each other when she had been supporting him through his ordeal of understanding and coping with his post-traumatic stress disorder. It had developed as a result of losing his leg and his left hand in an explosion during his tour of duty with the army. When other sources of help and support offered had not been enough, he had been referred to the charity Lila was working.

I was very happy for her. I'm not sure if it's really correct for a doctor to refer to his patient as pretty, but she really was very beautiful. I think the real beauty came from her bright and positive thinking and attitude, her refusal to be a victim and her caring and generous nature.

I remember early on when she once came to see me regarding headaches and tiredness, and having first excluded other possible causes like anaemia, for example, or an under-active thyroid gland, I mentioned it could be a symptom of depression. She would have none of it. It was then that I had my first glimpse of her way of thinking and through her stories about her family and her friends, her hopes, her dreams, even her confessed limitations of fully understanding certain things in life. She was a very inspiring person.

Despite the pressures of time in general practice, I have to admit I enjoyed her stories and never tried to interrupt her.

During one consultation, she told me about her beloved cat and described the way the cat made Lila love her. She never scratched her, was always there to welcome her home, always slept near her and was a wonderful companion. She was also a great source of entertainment to her.

Then the conversation turned to her boyfriend Tony and how much she loved him and her happiness whenever she could do something for him or support him in any issue. She then spoke lovingly about her older sister Rebecca, of whom she was so protective due to her moody husband. Always so much to give — that was Lila through and through.

Months passed by and Lila came to discuss the matter of contraception, but only for the short term, as she hinted that she and Tony were planning to start a family. She asked whether it was possible for paralysed women to have a baby.

I explained it was indeed possible but that her care would be specially tailored to her circumstances and that the delivery should be in hospital, to deal with any possible complications. I also reassured her that she would make a wonderful mother.

About eight months later, she and Tony came to me to discuss their plans in more detail and I was happy to give them my support. When later I was able to pass on to Lila the good news of a positive pregnancy test, I also invited her to see the nurse for a check-up, a prescription for folic acid and gave her the midwife's contact number.

I kept an eye on Lila throughout her antenatal care and the usual pregnancy issues. Then the hospital maternity unit wrote to tell me Lila had had a baby girl.

I saw little Nancy eight weeks later with Lila and Tony. She was a lovely, happy little one, who Lila brought in for every regular baby check. It was also a time for checking how Lila and Tony were coping with the usual sleepless nights and the baby's odd cold and cough that can seem so worrying to all first-time parents. Nancy seemed to not only have inherited her mum's lovely wide bright eyes, but also her determination.

Nancy grew up fast and was soon at nursery. Lila came to tell me that she and Tony had decided to have another little one for Nancy to play with and not to feel lonely. Before long, little Suzie arrived to join the happy family.

One day Lila came to discuss some muscular pain she was having and mentioned that Tony had got a job as an administrative officer in the Territorial Army in the north of England. She seemed unsure about this move and asked my opinion about it. I looked her in the eyes and advised her to trust her very good judgment that had so far never let her down.

I have to admit it was a bitter-sweet piece of news when, a couple of months later, the time came for the family to move away and the surgery received a lovely complimentary e-card thanking us for all the help they had received from the staff and wishing us well. We replied, wishing her all the best in her new life.

It is sad to see wonderful people like her and her lovely family going away, but it is also a privilege and inspiration to have had the chance to share their lives.

Chapter 12

Ms Footsie's golden advice

I USED to hate the endless junk mail that landed on my desk, but as I started to learn about coping with it, by recycling or using the back as scrap paper for writing notes, I found it useful. This story was written initially on the back of some of those scraps of paper.

This patient was a lawyer; a well-spoken lady in her early 30s, working for a prestigious legal firm dealing with the banking sector and the stock exchange in the city. She used to tell me about the city and her mixed group of clients, including the bankers and city traders. So I used to think of her as Ms Footsie (as in the FTSE Index).

She came one day with a small shopping list of issues; the contraceptive pill, a blood pressure check, itchiness in the armpit, and some painkillers for occasional knee pain. The issue of the knee pain reminded me of her last visit, during which she surprised me with brief story which one might give the title of "the healing power of prayer".

As she was having her lunch in one of the city's many sandwich bars, she noticed in front of her an elderly man with long braided hair and a Caribbean flag-coloured hat and wrist bands. Before he left he approached her and said: "Can I give you some advice, sister?"

A little surprised at this, but with time on her hands, she agreed to accept his offer.

He sat down at her table and they chatted for a few minutes. Then he casually asked her: "Do you get pain in the knees?"

She answered directly: "Yes, my knee has been bothering me for some time now!"

The subject changed and after a little more general chat he rose to leave. Before he did, he asked her permission to touch her knee and say some prayers. She agreed and afterwards he disappeared out of the shop into the busy crowd.

She was so surprised at this that she had not even thought to protest. But what was more amazing was that the pain that had nagged for so long was nearly gone.

When she came to me she was puzzled about how he had known she had been in pain. She was so impressed that I resisted saying it was probably that, un-noticed by herself, when she was pulling out her chair to sit down she may have twisted her knee and winced.

Sadly the effect of the prayers on her pain was short-lived, so she was back to see me with knee pain. She also reminded me of her chronic back pain and incidentally mentioned she was travelling to Africa soon to act as prosecution in a case for her brother, who had been physically assaulted by another trader. He had taken her brother's goods (he traded second-hand TV sets, which he shipped from the UK) and hadn't paid him for them. When her brother protested he was beaten and left for dead.

Finally she requested a one-week sick note as her back and knee pain were playing up. At this point I think she remembered we had a passionate debate about this before, during which I had advised her about the issue of her weight making matters worse for her.

She also knew from previous experience that I was not at all convinced by the all too common exclamations (which I had heard on many occasions from many people): "But doctor, I don't eat anything and I just put on weight!"

When I highlighted to her that we were now facing a national problem where obesity affects more than a quarter of our population, she vigorously defended her claim as if she had found herself back in a court.

She proceeded to lecture me and to enlighten me with her golden advice about how she had lost weight and it was something I should pass on to all my obese patients.

She explained that she had tried everything on earth and nothing had worked for her, including all published types of diet and joining many slimming clubs. She reminded me the free fat-busting medications on the NHS hadn't work either. According to our revered NICE (National Institute for Health and care Excellence) guidelines, I'd had to stop these after a period of time with no progress.

Ms Footsie had then tried a new technique she'd adopted recently, a type of yoga called Chakra, based on the seven energy centres of the body. She frequently tried to educate me about this alternative method, mentioning the names of these energy centres and their actions and the co-ordination between the body and the mind.

I appreciated her efforts and was very clear she was convinced, but all the time I was thinking if this was really the right time and what would my poor patients in the waiting room be thinking now? On the other hand, I was in no position to judge whether or not this might be the magic solution in the future for my patients.

After she finished her lecture she added to this technique a certain prayer which she had been using (apparently) very successfully for the past six months and all her friends and family praised her for her transformation.

As I said, we'd had this debate all too often. I had discussed with her the increased risk of heart disease, diabetes, stroke and cancer and had offered her all the right advice, from keeping a food diary, multiple diet sheets, referral to weight management programs and the dietician at the hospital, and referral to the Healthwise programme for increasing physical activity under supervision. Nothing seemed to have worked.

I decided I'd had enough and that the weighing scales would not lie. So I invited her for a reality check and to stand on my 'scales of justice'. I promised I wouldn't look. But I heard her exclaim in pained tones: "Oh no, my God!"

I had not expected such an agonised response to the inevitable result, so I quickly went to see what had happened and to console her.

"Ms Footsie, one-hundred! You seem to have gone up from 97 kilos since our last check," I said sadly. "I would highly recommend that you need to review this Chakra yoga and prayers method."

She looked so heartbroken that I added: "But I am very grateful to you for educating me so thoroughly about the alternative approach and I will keep your golden advice in mind."

I issued her prescription for the requested painkillers and the sick note, asking her to return before her journey to Africa for a review and a serious chat. I also gave her another copy of the diet record sheet and asked her to complete it honestly and bring it with her next time.

Ms Footsie came back few months later, after her trip, to discuss the surgical option for her weight, backed with a host of articles from the internet and stories from her friends and family.

I tried to explain fairly the risks and the possible complications versus the benefits. Surgery was really only the very last resort, if all other methods had been seriously tried. I added that any referral would be to see a dietician first. It was part of the preparation for the surgical procedure (called Bariatric surgery) to assess obese people and to determine whether they were suitable for it. She went away to think about it.

Some months passed by and I came across a letter informing me she had turned up at Accident & Emergency with abdominal pain and bouts of diarrhoea as she had decided to have the bariatric surgery done in Belgium. When she rang them about her deteriorating condition, according to their post-operative care protocol, they advised her to go to A&E and for our free NHS to pick up the pieces.

Thankfully, with the good care of the NHS, she recovered from her misadventures and after a while returned to see me at the surgery.

Ms Footsie requested copies of her investigations and letters from her medical record, as she had decided to move back to Africa to establish an international law firm to make a stand against the corrupted officials of the government there.

I admired her bravery and reflected how this service was much needed in many parts of the world, not just Africa. I wished her the very best of luck, as she would most definitely need it with this massive mission. I hope she was successful, or at least made some positive impact with her aspirations. However, I am sorry to say that I never found out.

For more information visit www.nhs.uk/conditions/obesity

Chapter 13

Good deeds

JOHN and his wife Gail had moved to our area years ago and I came to know them shortly after they had registered with the practice. I remember clearly the first consultation with John, an ordinary-looking, well-spoken Englishman in his early 50s.

He had come to get his blood pressure checked and probably familiarise himself with the surgery before he brought his wife with him. Gail had, after a series of long investigations, been diagnosed with motor neurone disease and due to the weakness in her legs was confined to a wheelchair. Despite this, she was an independent lady and didn't let her disability get in the way of life for her and her husband.

As is usual with newly registered patients, I asked John about his smoking and drinking history. He told me he used to smoke around 40 cigarettes a day and had been drinking heavily for about 10 years. Then he paused, adding that he had since stopped both habits.

John continued: "After I was treated for my smoking and drinking I developed depression and became homeless for some time – I don't wish to remember how long it was before I found my feet again, thanks to the Lord and my dear wife Gail."

He used to be a very successful broker for a reputable estate agent that exclusively dealt with multi-million pound properties, but with the pressure of the job and the emergence of professional jealousy came a change in lifestyle. John spent long days at work and left very little time for his previous wife, and their relationship slowly become more distant.

The symptoms of anxiety and depression caused by his job were attended to by a private doctor, but a routine of late-night meetings, endless voicemails, messages and mounting pressure from ever-nearing deadlines led to an increase in his smoking and drinking habits.

His then wife's only source of comfort and sanity came from her work colleagues, as she was unable to talk to her husband most of the time. The situation worsened with the advent of the financial crisis and a slowed economy as John was made redundant and spent his days sitting at home and drinking.

One day his wife came home and confessed to him that she was having an affair and it was unethical for them to remain married. Hit with a devastating divorce, John was unfairly left with all but nothing to his name and found himself homeless. He felt so ashamed of his sad circumstances and did not want to worry his mother Unsure of what to do, he stayed with an old work friend for a few days before deciding to sleep in the park with only a sleeping bag, a box of biscuits and some loose change in his pocket.

"Sad memories," he said to me.

I sympathised with his story and concluded the consultation as I felt John had been reminded enough about his painful past. I explained that his blood pressure was high and advised him to avoid stress and long shifts at work, to sleep well and come back in two weeks for a check-up.

As I typed in the blood test request I heard him telling himself in a voice tinged with irony to 'avoid stress!' I agreed with him, life could make that difficult, but it was important.

He replied: "I know, but it is hard, doc, as Gail's condition is deteriorating slowly in front of my eyes and I feel helpless."

I interrupted him gently and asked: "When am I going to see her?"

He said that he would try to book an appointment for next week. I handed him the blood form and, with a mutual smile, wished him good luck.

Two weeks later, I saw their names on my list: a double appointment for Gail as she was in a wheelchair and one for John. My recommendation to reception is always to book extended appointments for our less able patients as they usually have multiple medical problems to be reviewed.

They entered the consultation room with a smile. I introduced myself to Gail and quickly noticed how frail she was. I was surprised that although she looked as if she might be in her late 60s, her actual age on the computer record put her in her mid-50s. But the other striking feature was how clear the emotional bond between them was, especially with John's care and the loving tenderness he showed towards her.

Gail mentioned that she had been diagnosed with motor neurone disease some time ago and was feeling weaker month by month, despite getting all the support she needed from John and two private nursing carers on a daily basis.

She seemed to be very articulate and knowledgeable about her condition and so had a high expectation from the medical profession. I asked about her eating, her sleeping, her mood and any other needs.

As I gave her the repeat medications and requested some base line blood tests, she asked if she could have them done after a week . She then explained that they were going to visit John's mother in Devon for a few days. John added that he needed to visit his mother because they did combined charity work for homeless people each year around Christmas time. Of course I had no objection.

I looked after both of them for quite some time and got to know them very well. Months and years passed by with ordinary consultations for sore throats, shoulder pains and other common illnesses.

Then one day I saw a message from John requesting some phone advice. I called him at the end of the session and he told me Gail was suffering from a bad cough and couldn't sleep at night. She wasn't eating and was feeling very unwell. Worried, I decided to visit her.

I arrived at a large electric-gated detached house, with a well-tended front garden. John ushered me into Gail's room upstairs. I had a brief chat, examined her, gave her treatment for a chest infection and left her to sleep. Coming down the stairs I felt John wanted to tell me something and that he may need a listening ear for a few minutes.

He offered me a cup of tea, saying he had just put the kettle on to have one himself. I accepted his offer, admitting to my bad habit of sugar in my tea. John showed me into the fabulous conservatory, with a tastefully decorated sitting area filled with healthy plants.

I complimented John about the lovely atmosphere and he started to tell me it was all under the management of his wife, with the help and organisation of an efficient house-keeper and a gardener. He admitted that it might seem a great expense but finance wasn't a problem for them, as Gail had inherited money from her parents.

However, he added that money couldn't buy everything, especially good health. Despite their financial security, John still liked to do some work to keep himself active ,by working as a taxi driver.

As I started explaining the expected deterioration in Gail's health in the future and the increasing needs she would have, John read my mind and understood what would be coming in the weeks and months ahead.

Suddenly, with a sad gaze, looking away from me and staring at the garden and the clear sky, John recalled when he had first met Gail. He was homeless and sitting near a Tube station entrance, asking people for some change. One day he noticed this lovely lady who used to buy coffee from the shop next to the station and would sometimes buy biscuits or chocolate for him.

She used to smile at statements John would write on pieces of paper, such as 'life is unpredictable' or 'I used to have a house like yours but I lost it, so please help'.

Then one cold day in early December, Gail came with a cup of tea for him and a sympathetic smile. John was standing with the station manager, who knew him from the early days when they used to play darts together at a local pub.

Gail asked the station manager about the engineering works over the weekend, as she had important meetings in the city near Christmas time.

"As he told her about the timetable changes she smiled at me and asked me if I was OK." John smiled at the memory "It was the most pleasant and warm question I had received for some time. We had a brief chat and then she rushed to catch the train."

Just before Christmas, Gail gave John some warm clothes and a few addresses of places that could provide him with a meal, a bath and some shelter. John followed up her suggestions and would see her every morning and evening, to say hello and thank her.

He said he used to wonder around and then sit in the small park in front of the station, reading the free papers left around, until he would see Gail coming out.

One day she invited him for a cup of tea and a sandwich on her way home. They talked a lot and after hearing John's story, she told him about her own very bad experience a long time ago with a repeatedly cheating partner. They broke up and she never wanted to repeat the experience again.

However, the relationship between John and Gail blossomed with lots of understanding, respect, caring and then love for each other.

I went back to the surgery and reflected about what John had said and agreed that life can be cruel sometimes: you can't have everything, you win some and you lose some!

Many weeks later, Gail's condition deteriorated one weekend and according to a previous discussion with her and her expressed wishes, she refused to go to hospital, choosing instead to die in peace in the loving surrounding of her home. She passed away in her sleep, with her dear husband and beloved dog beside her.

I rang John and paid him my condolences and invited him to see me when he was ready for any support he needed. After about a week he came to the surgery and was naturally very sad and depressed. I requested urgent counselling from a bereavement service called Cruse.

A few months later, I found his name on my session list. He came for his blood pressure medication and asked me for some help with his sleep. He would go to bed as usual at around 11pm, but would then keep on tossing and turning until 3 or 4 in the morning, with vivid memories of the past hanging from the ceiling (as he described them). I gave him some medication to help him and advice about improving his sleep.

He returned a few months later with a cold and cough. During the appointment he mentioned that he got it from the change of weather when he went to see his mother in Devon, where it was rainy and windy. However, he expressed relief that he'd been able to talk about the death of Gail to his mother.

John said he needed to visit his mother more frequently as she was getting frailer with every visit he made. He smiled as he told me how he had taken his mother out for a meal, and they bumped into a very old friend of hers. She and his mother had worked together and that day she had her daughter Angela with her. Angela had been at school with John and had been very cheeky and used to tease him. They were soon in deep conversation about school memories.

What a small world, he thought. Angela had apparently left England to settle in Italy, near Turin. She enjoyed life there with her husband and her adopted eight-year-old son Emanuel. Sadly she had lost her husband three years earlier and found it difficult to continue in Italy without him. So she decided to be near her mother and her two sisters. Angela was happy that Emanuel had got used to the school and the changes and had settled in well.

John was glad to have seen Angela again and they agreed to continue the hard work of his mother's charity together, to take the load off his mother. So John started to visit Devon every month to continue the good work.

I was very happy to see John moving on from his bereavement and sadness, and we agreed he should return in a few months for blood pressure and general checks.

However, it was about six months before he came back. He happily told me he was spending a lot of time with Angela and had even moved in temporarily with her to keep an eye on his ailing mother.

Things went well and a few months later John came to have his routine medical for his Taxi licence. He said he was selling his house and moving to Devon.

He was so grateful for all the support and care of the staff and thanked all our team with a lovely card and chocolates. He was so enthusiastic about the move and continuing the good deeds of his mother, looking after the homeless.

His passion to do good was clearly inherited from his mother and although I did not know her, I felt great respect and admiration for her.

I smiled at John and the phrase that came to mind was 'Do good and good will come to you'. John had certainly worked hard to earn his happiness, although like many good people he would not have seen it that way; it was just part of his nature.

Cruse Bereavement Care – Tel: 0808 808 1677
Crisis (Homeless) – Tel: 0300 636 1967

Chapter 14

The lady in red

MANY people have a distinct appearance which might be said to be 'once seen, never forgotten'. I will call this lady Mrs Scarlet, as she always dressed in very flattering shades of red, and you could say she fell into this category.

I first met her when she was in her early 60s and she had taken early retirement as an assistant teacher. She used to tell me about the teaching profession, how it was in the past and how it was now, in schools all over our country.

Despite this subject being away from the context of our consultations, it was of great interest to me to know about the conditions of work from people actually on the frontline of education.

Amongst my patients I have a dozen or so teachers and assistant head teachers and their stories have helped me to understand why many of them are so unhappy in their working environment. To an outsider it may seem odd because our politicians often seem to declare how committed they are to this vital field ('Education, education, education!'), much like the way they speak so often of their efforts to protect our beloved NHS.

Maybe this is why I have found such a lot in common between our two professions − with targets, tick-boxes, guidelines, constraints on our professional skills and increasingly unbearable levels of stress.

Their struggles to deliver a positive educational experience in the face of rapidly declining appreciation and respect for their years of experience from students, parents and the government have a taken a terrible toll.

Disillusionment, combined with stress, anxiety, and severe depression, has driven ever larger numbers of dedicated teachers out of a profession they once loved, at a time when they are needed most. The parallels with the medical profession are quite stark.

Mrs Scarlet, our pleasant lady in red, also used to tell me about many aspects of her life since retirement. She was a keen voluntary worker for many good causes, including working for charities for the homeless and orphaned children.

I was also aware of her life's struggle in raising her three daughters alone after the sudden loss of her young husband to a massive heart attack, all of whom became university graduates and are now leading very successful lives. It was a difficult time financially and the family made ends meet through selling cakes at weekend car boot sales.

She was a well-spoken lady, a good thinker, very sensible and observant, and these characteristics gave me the idea that she would make an excellent member of our surgery Patient Participation Group (PPG). This group was formed to meet quarterly to give patients a chance to raise questions, concerns and suggestions to improve the way the practice provided services and cared for them and their families.

I was delighted that Mrs Scarlet agreed and she was eager to contact our practice manager to put the next date in her diary. As promised, she attended her first meeting and was introduced to the other members.

At first Mrs Scarlet was a bit shy and just observed the proceedings. The meeting was very democratic, with every-one being able to express their views. However, certain topics, such as politics, religion or football, were banned as these sometimes ended up with passionate disagreements that would distract from the purpose of the meeting.

Mrs Scarlet waited until we had reached the last item on the agenda; A.O.B (any other business). At this point she produced a little piece of paper with three items on it. She mentioned each point briefly, then waited for me to respond.

The first point concerned the increasing number of patients who didn't attend their appointment or didn't bother to ring in advance to cancel them. We record the figures each week in the hope that people will become aware how many appointments are lost through this thoughtlessness. Mrs Scarlet wanted to know how this problem could be tackled.

I agreed this was a very important point and would put it on our next agenda, reporting back on actions the practice had been able to take.

The other two points were related to our local hospital and I said I would also add these to our next agenda.

After we had finished the meeting, Mrs Scarlet noticed that I had gone to the kitchen to quickly have my caffeine fix before another meeting and my evening session. She came over for a brief chat about the weather forecast and the state of the NHS.

After a few meetings this little chat became routine, and one day Mrs Scarlet cornered me in the kitchen, this time asking for an explanation as to why she was hearing repeatedly in the news that many hospitals in the country were in the red?

I kept stirring the sugar in my cup and, trying to lighten the tone of this serious matter, I said that some people liked the colour the red as it was the colour of love and affection.

Mrs Scarlet peered over her rectangular glasses, every inch the disapproving teacher, and said that it was certainly not the case for hospitals and that their debt had been running unaddressed for many years!

I tried hard to avoid this ambiguous debate, as I had been through it on many occasions, with either a poor outcome or no outcome at all.

I looked at her and said: "You know, when I was in training in the hospital many years ago, I took many points with me on the road of life. During my mental health training I noticed that a team of doctors would try to tell the unfortunate patient that he or she was ill and needed help and treatment. If the patient didn't have an insight on their condition they would not accept the diagnosis and sometimes would even accuse the doctors of being mentally ill themselves. So here is the problem of lack of insight. Despite the great effort of the very hard-working staff under extreme conditions the NHS doesn't want to recognise that it has a chronic problem called 'redness' or debt through mismanagement and this condition needs serious treatment. Even if it was prescribed treatment, it would probably come up with 101 excuses for not taking it."

I then added, smiling at the memory: "There was a common joke before I left the hospital training that a patient on the operating table was surrounded by many people. In the corner of the theatre a member of the clinical team was asking another what they were waiting for. The other one said. 'The surgeon'. So his confused colleague asked 'who are all these people then?' To his surprise the answer came back, 'the MANAGERS, of course!'"

One day, when I was a junior doctor, I was running an outpatient clinic and was writing a few lines to the patient's GP for the patient to take with him. I was looking for an envelope to put the letter in, but couldn't find one. This seemed odd as there always used to be plenty of stationery on these desks. So I went out to ask the outpatient nurse, who came to search for one and then stopped, remembering that all the stationery had been locked in a cupboard. Unfortunately, the new stationery manager was off sick that day and she had the only keys. The nurse offered to go and get an envelope from the secretaries in the fourth floor, but as we were, as usual, short of staff and it really wasn't her job anyway, I declined this kind offer.

In the end I had no choice but to give the patient the folded letter without an envelope and apologised to him and his GP.

After I finished the clinic I asked the nurse why we had changed the system. She raised an eyebrow, smiled and said that because the hospital managers thought that some staff were taking some of the stationery home and this was costing the hospital money. So they appointed a new manager to look after the stationery – the 'logic' being to appoint a manager for a salary of thousands of pounds ... to save the hospital a few pennies.

When I told this story to Mrs Scarlet I explained this was the disease called "penny wise, pound foolish", for which it seemed the NHS had no cure.

By now, Mrs Scarlet understood very well what I meant and I kept enjoying the sips of my caffeine fix, reminiscing about my days in the hospital. It also made me a little sad to remember these stories and realise that no lessons had been learnt and things had not got better but worse.

Mrs Scarlet came in between the quarterly PPG meetings to check her blood pressure and to pick up a prescription for her medications, as she was going up north to see one of her daughters. She told me that they would be going for a break in the Lake District. With so many wonderful places in Britain to visit, she wondered why it was that people felt the need to go abroad.

While I was preparing her prescription she explained that some of her tablets came in packs of 28, while other tablets came in packs of 30. This meant after a few months she would end up with a mismatch – too many of some or not enough of others.

She asked if I could change them to the same amount of each, so she would only have to come in once a month for her prescription.

I asked if she preferred 28 or 30. She said it did not matter as long as they were all the same amount. Then she explained that giving her a two-month supply of 28 tablets made it 56, and a two-month supply of 30 tablets made it 60, meaning the 56 tablets would finish before the 60s. So she would need to request a new prescription for both and would each month end up with another four extra from the latter. After a few months there would be many unused tablets, which seemed a terrible waste.

I was already aware of this common problem, especially for my patients on many medications. I was often asked to synchronise the tablets, but due to the different pack sizes and the different dosages it wasn't long before they were all out of step again.

I told Mrs Scarlet to leave it with me while she was away and I would report back to her when we next met.

A few days later, between the morning and afternoon sessions, with no interruptions from phone calls, staff or any other unpredictable events, I found myself drafting an email to the Department of Health explaining the observation of medication box discrepancies and the long-term effect on patients, staff and the pharmacies, not to mention the huge potential cost to the NHS of wasted medication (only adding to the terrible debt described earlier).

Several days later, I received a reply, acknowledging there was a waste of medications, which cost the NHS more than £100 million a year, and that my observations were part of this issue.

However, they didn't mention a solution to this problem. I was not totally satisfied with this response, but pleased they had at least agreed with my observations. I decided to raise it at the next PPG meeting with our lady in red.

Mrs Scarlet was impressed, but she frowned as she spotted there had been no attempt at finding a solution for the problem. She kept looking at me and I tried to avoid her gaze, as I knew she was asking me for more action on this front.

The best I could do, as the Department of Health seemed to have no interest, was to ask the suppliers of the various clinical software systems to see if they could come up with a programme to do the calculations for proper synchronisation. They responded that they were also aware of the issue and had plans to address it in the future. All we could do was to wait and see.

Thankfully, both Mrs Scarlet and myself forgot about this topic for a while, as we were discussing other nagging issues regarding the patients and the surgery and the ailing condition of the NHS across the country.

One day, Mrs Scarlet asked if there was any voluntary work she could do for the surgery, as she had a few hours free. I asked her if she would agree to chair a monthly meeting for a few patients who had multiple chronic diseases, such as diabetes, respiratory disease, heart disease and high blood pressure.

Mrs Scarlet agreed with enthusiasm and the feedback from the patients was brilliant. She had printed out information sheets about their conditions and what they could do to help themselves, adding real-life stories of similar patients from the internet. Her enthusiasm and pro-active attitude was infectious and had a very positive impact on our patients.

Mrs Scarlet was and still is a great asset to her family and everybody who knows her, and we hope to see her in this fine form for many years to come.

Chapter 15

Call me what you like (Miss Mori)

MY next patient was a new face. Checking my computer screen, I read Miss Morioriojurer-eolu-wagba*. But things started off a little muddled.

I smiled and introduced myself. "Good morning, I'm Dr Moss. How do you do?"

"I'm a student," she replied.

Trying to avoid further misunderstanding or appearing rude in mispronouncing her somewhat challenging name, I tried again.

"How may I address you?"

She looked at me sharply. "I've given my address to the reception already."

Sinking rapidly and keen to move on to our consultation, I tried another way.

"What name would you like me to use? What can I call you?"

She raised an eyebrow, so I quickly volunteered: "Can I call you Miss Mori?"

She shrugged. "Call me what you like."

It was not a promising start, but I got to know her better over the years, as she usually left me with one or two question marks or a frown.

However, this first consultation seemed to set the tone, as did her first request.

She related her story as follows. Miss Mori came to this very hospitable country, like many others, to study English on a student visa from Africa. She enrolled with a school, registered at our clinic and made her first appointment.

She was short and stout, but also clearly very overweight (obese, curvy or dimensionally challenged − call it what you like!). Despite her heavily accented and broken English, her pronounced facial features carried a strong attitude of determination, and altogether she presented a formidable force as she gave me her requirements.

"We had a test at school last month and I didn't go. I want a sick note for that day."

I tried to explain that this was the first time we had met and doctors cannot to give backdated sick notes without evidence of sickness.

"You should have reported to the clinic that you were unwell at the time, then we would have a record," I told her.

"But you were not my doctor then!" she replied.

Before I could continue she launched into her next concern.

"OK then, you see, doctor, I'm big and I try to lose some weight. I don't eat much but still putting on weight! My friends said doctors can give you slimming pills. Can I have slimming tablets?"

I sighed inwardly at this all-too-familiar tale. I then had to spend some considerable time advising her about changes to diet and activity levels that would have to be tried before I could consider prescribing any slimming tablets, this being very clear in the clinical guidelines our profession follows. She was clearly unconvinced and ignored my references to diet, activity or guidelines.

Instead she moved on swiftly to tell me she was working as a part-time cleaner as well as doing her studies. Then, with a big smile, she swiftly offered to clean our clinic. I firmly refused her offer, explaining we already had a very good cleaning company taking care of that.

However, she wasn't giving up that easily, repeating the offer and adding that she would do it much cheaper than any company. Feeling myself being dragged into unnecessary negotiations, I had to firmly push the subject back to the task in hand.

"I'll ask the dietician to send you an appointment to review your diet and to see if she can help. You can talk to the practice manager about the cleaning proposal if you want to. Have a nice day!"

But she wasn't finished with me yet.

"OK, doctor, can I have some free condoms? A friend of mine told me you can get them free on the NHS."

"I'm sorry, I don't keep these in my consultation room. You will have to ask our nurse."

I then deliberately turned to my computer to start writing her consultation into her notes. Then I noticed the flagged reminder to confirm her address and phone number. Could it really have changed between registration and first appointment?

As she was still glued to her seat I decided to quickly ask her about her address (something I was soon to regret!).

With a subtle grin she said: "Oh, this is not my address, this is my friend's address. But she said I can use it."

I then noticed there were three different mobile phone numbers too and when I asked about these she said one was hers and the other two belonged to her friends, as they could pass on messages to her if we contacted them.

Miss Mori was already pulling out her mobile phone from her bag, explaining that it was old and had poor reception, as it was free from one of her friends. She insisted that when she could buy a new one with very good reception, the clinic could contact her on that as well.

"I'm sorry, but because of data protection we are not allowed to discuss patient information with other people. We have to protect patient confidentiality." I tried to explain.

"What is this word 'con-fi-den-ti-a-li-ty, doctor?" She very carefully pronounced every syllable with an expression of suspicion on her face.

I wracked my poor brain to find a simple way to convey the meaning of the tight regulations we were bound by and the implications. It was even something our patients were asked to evaluate us on in the annual Patient Survey. Unfortunately, there are some patients who don't understand the word and some tick the wrong box by mistake. This then gives a poor impression and can result in a surgery having to explain itself for failing their patients!

Another compulsory patient survey of satisfaction with consultations/service (Friends & Family) regularly throws up glowing words of appreciation followed by a box ticked 'would not recommend to friends and family' because the form has been misunderstood!

This reminds of a similar experience I had with our annual GP appraisal (a peer review of our fitness to practice). Part of the process is that a random selection of patients must be asked to complete a tick-box questionnaire to give their view on their doctor's performance in different areas. Again the complexity/subtlety of the questions can confuse patients who have a weaker grasp of the English language and can result in a very contradictory picture of the doctor's performance – which can raise awkward questions during the appraisal.

This only adds to the onerous burden of the appraisal process, where a doctor is asked to complete a huge file of evidence and answer endless questions to prove he/she is fit to continue his/her job.

On one occasion I remember a colleague telling me he had been interrogated about his probity (essentially openness to bribery and corruption!) when he honestly declared that a patient had given him a small gift (a picture frame) in gratitude for going the extra mile. You can perhaps understand how all this bureaucracy distracts us unnecessarily from the medicine we trained so hard to perform, adding workload and stress to an already overstretched profession.

Back to Miss Mori, who had by now left my room. I thought I had sorted everything out when I heard a commotion going on in reception. Tentatively I poked my head around my door to check what was going on, only to see Miss Mori having a very heated debate with our nurse.

"Only four! That is not enough and I need coloured ones!"

Guessing the topic of this difference of opinion, I quietly withdrew my head and closed the door, knowing my staff were more than capable of sorting this out, God bless them.

A few months later, Miss Mori returned with a sore throat and cough, which she'd had for a few days. I examined her throat and chest, both were fine, and her temperature was normal. It was just a minor viral illness, so I reassured her and advised gargling with salt water and drinking some honey, lemon and ginger.

She looked at me doubtfully and with a little frown said: "My friend said I need antibiotics."

"No, there's no need for an antibiotics," I replied firmly.

"OK, doctor. But I need a three-week sick note because I can't work or study like this."

Reluctantly I decided to write a sick note.

"But one week is enough, and if you are still not well you can come back for another check. If it is needed I may be able to give another week, but I doubt that this will be the case."

While I was preparing the sick note I heard her complaining,

"All my body paining me and I feel I need total body massage."

I ignored what I had heard, but turned to find her asking in all seriousness: "Do you do total body massage on the NHS?"

Not sure if she was asking me personally I told her firmly: "No, I don't do total body massage on the NHS! You need to find a privately advertised service."

"But I cannot afford that! I have no money," she replied indignantly.

"Maybe your friends could help...." I started, but she wasn't going to leave empty-handed.

"I need a letter for the food bank, so I can get some free food."

It was quite a long time before I saw Miss Mori again, and I had almost forgotten her and her name. However, seeing her name on my list one day brought all the memories flooding back.

"Good morning, doctor!"

Hoping she would not cloud my previously relatively good day I greeted her with a smile. "Yes, it is a very good and sunny morning, Miss Mori!" I answered. To my surprise she gave an even bigger smile.

"I have good news, doctor. I'm pregnant ... and I want a letter to the council to put my name on the waiting list for a flat."

I congratulated her and requested an early-morning urine sample to send to the laboratory for a pregnancy test.

"Why, doctor?" she said. "I know I'm pregnant, a woman can tell!"

"I agree but our protocol is to send a sample to the laboratory to be formally confirmed." I explained. "You see, we once had a very kind locum doctor, who had a patient who said she was pregnant. She gave the lady a letter that she was pregnant to her work and later we discovered she was not pregnant and the practice was questioned about it. So it is safer this way."

"But I cannot wait for that, I need my letter today," she insisted. "I feel sick every morning and I need a sick note for one month."

I shook my head. "You need to report to your employer first, it's called self-certification. You don't need a sick note until there has been one week of sickness. Call back for your pregnancy test results in two to three days."

Exactly three days later she returned for her positive pregnancy test, got her housing letter, a sick note for morning sickness and a letter confirming her pregnancy. She was given advice and three months of Folic acid (free on the NHS!).

I hinted that the letters she had requested were not part of the free NHS service and she would need to pay a small fee at reception for them.

She frowned and asked how much. When I said £10, to cover the time and work of producing the letter, she answered: "£10! This is not a small fee! I'm a student and can't afford it, and I'm pregnant."

I advised her that it was the same for all such letters, and to ask the reception staff to explain the rules to her.

Most patients seem quite unaware that doctors are not obliged to write non-medical letters for them and this is not in our NHS contract or paid for by the NHS. This is additional work for our staff and we need to charge for it. Not everything is 'free on the NHS'.

Miss Mori left to continue her debate with reception and I glanced at my list to see who was next. This patient had not arrived yet, and by the name I knew he would either be very late or more probably not turn up. If he came he would end up shouting at staff because he would have to wait until the end of the session to be seen or rebook for another day. This was only fair as otherwise his carelessness would make other people's appointments run late, when they had arrived in good time. But of course he would not see it like that. To be honest, the doctor concerned did not have to see him, after all if you are late for a train, does it have to wait for you?

The problem is that if a doctor is running late in his appointments (because other patients have taken more than their 10 minutes due to a serious diagnosis or complex problem, or an emergency phone call had to be taken) then there are often complaints against us. But if a patient turns up late they often expect to be seen there and then, and who cares if others are affected by their action.

We keep a weekly list of the numbers of appointments lost from patients simply not turning up and not letting us know if they no longer need their appointments. Most weeks we can lose over 40 appointments this way, which can rapidly add up to almost 200 a month — appointments that could have been given to those who really needed them.

We publish these figures on our noticeboards and website, hoping people will see the consequences. Ironically, it is often the worst offenders who complain most when there is no appointment when they want one!

While I was thinking like that, I heard a knock on my door. It was our senior and very tolerant receptionist, Kate. Unusually for her, she was very flustered. I asked her to sit and tell me the problem.

"I'm sorry, I know you are very busy, but I am having a big problem convincing one of your patients to pay her fee. I really don't understand these people. They say they have no money, but they have two mobile phones and the most recent, expensive ones too, better than mine!" She paused before adding: "And I know you would not tell her the fee was only £5."

I shook my head. "No, I didn't."

I really understood her frustration, and tried to reassure her she was doing fine. So Kate went out to continue the difficult negotiation and I called my next patient.

I did not hear about the outcome of this issue, but a few weeks later Miss Mori was back in my room. She was asking for another sick note as her back was aching and it made it impossible to work. She also requested help with getting her Sure Start Vouchers (for free milk and supplements) in preparation for her baby's arrival.

I asked if she was otherwise well and whether she was getting any support from her partner or friends.

She laughed and said: "I don't know where the father is. It was one night only and probably he is not in the country. He was drunk and told me that he needed to go back to Africa to change his passport. You know, he said he conned many people and the bank, and the police are after him."

She paused a little, then after some thought added: "Probably not, as the police doesn't bother to chase people unless it is a million pounds and above, and my partner only conned the bank for £400,000."

I was quite speechless as this was not exactly what I had expected to hear, and not with such apparently unconcerned openness.

She seemed to be waiting for a response and maybe my silence made her think I doubted her story. So she continued: "You know, doctor, here in London the police is aware of a complete street where many houses are involved in scams and fraud, but the police don't have the thingy....you know the word they use... resorts?"

"Resources?" I said faintly.

"Yes, resources," she continued. "The police have given the street a nickname of an African city. It's true, doctor," she insisted. "If you need a passport or driving licence, just go there and ask anybody."

I declined, saying I had my passport and driving licence already thank you. I tried to change this sticky subject back to her health.

She said she was tired, so I suggested doing a blood test for anaemia and Vitamin D deficiency, but she said: "No, doctor, I think it's because I sleep rough."

"Why are you not sleeping well? I asked. "You need to get a good night's sleep."

To my surprise she answered: "Yes, I know. I might ask my friend to let me sleep in her house for a few days."

Realising she really meant 'sleeping rough', I said: "I thought you were living in your friend's house."

"No, that is my address for letters, but I live somewhere else. You are my doctor and I trust you and I'll tell you. You know the old boarded redbrick building after the fuel station and next to the police station?"

I nodded that I did. It was an empty council building, which a colleague had offered to buy from the council to open a drug and alcohol rehabilitation centre and other community services, which the area was in dire needed of. But the council had messed him around and he had given up.

Now it seemed the 'community' had put it to another use. Miss Mori mentioned that she had been invited to join the squatters there. She was delighted, as they apparently had access to free water and electricity, courtesy of knowledgeable people who knew how to attach a supply.

I provided the requested paperwork and she wished me a cheery goodbye, leaving me with a multitude of questions and concerns.

Some months passed, and I heard Miss Mori had delivered a healthy baby boy. She came for her six-week postnatal visit and I was introduced to baby Mori.

As is usual in these appointments, I raised the matter of contraception, but Miss Mori had her own agenda.

"I need a letter to the council now that I have a baby. He was born here, he is British and I need a flat soon, as I can't stay with friends. It has to be two bedrooms as he has to have his own room so I get a good night's sleep, as you advised me in the past."

The list continued, and she seemed very well informed of everything she was entitled to. Finally she produced from her bag a cutting from a magazine. It was an advertisement for an orthopaedic mattress.

"My back and my neck are aching after delivery and my friend said, 'See, it is written in the advertisement, you can get this orthopaedic mattress on the NHS'."

I advised her that I was not aware of this, but I could give her some painkillers and a referral to the physiotherapy team to help her with her back and neck pain. But she started to argue her case and because I felt I had no time or energy to continue this pointless debate, I decided to offer her another option.

"Unfortunately the NHS is very strict with our budget and these types of request need to be assessed on a case-by-case basis. I advise you to book with Dr Newman as she is our lead for such matters and you can discuss it with her."

I saw Dr Newman during the break and mentioned to her that as long as she sent few patients to me for a second opinion, then I was happy to return the favour and send her one, just one, if she didn't mind. Innocently, she agreed with a curious smile, asking about the case. I said that it would be best for her to judge herself, as it was a second and independent opinion.

Later in the week Dr Newman caught me in the corridor and thanked me for the referral, but said that in future she would prefer not to accept these types of referral from me. I felt a pang of guilt, but pointed out that this was her field. She frowned at me, but before she could protest I thanked her most sincerely and rushed off to my room, hoping this was an end to the matter.

I was wrong. A month later, Miss Mori came back with another request. This one, however, was a bit odd. She asked for a letter to the Home Office for herself, but she wanted it with a different name and a different date of birth!

"I'll explain, doctor. I came to England on a forged passport − it carries my surname but a different first name and different date of birth. But now I have my baby born here I want things to be corrected."

I said I could not do anything about it, but advised she put the request in writing to the practice manager and the health authority.

I warned her that the Home Office might not accept this, but she answered emphatically: "A solicitor from my home town used to work for the Home Office and he says that this will be against the human rights of my boy, and on family grounds I must stay too."

She stopped suddenly, as if she had forgotten something, and then added: "My boy is growing now and in the near future we may need a house with a garden for him to play in, so I will need a letter....."

"You can ask the manager for help with that too," I replied.

One morning, a while later, as I was taking a few letters to the staff in the reception, I saw Miss Mori.

I recognised her, from her back and her unmistakable voice, as she was talking to the reception staff. I was about to go back to my room, but out of foolish curiosity I changed my mind and approached reception.

I was talking to Kate the receptionist when I heard Miss Mori calling me.

"Doctor, doctor! See my beautiful boy! I am booking his injections with the nurse!"

She was beaming at me as she continued to tell me her news.

"I am so grateful to you, doctor. I have been given a house with a garden for my beautiful boy, and he has his own room too."

But briefly her smile faded.

"I am sorry, doctor, the house is not in London but in Kent, and I just heard from the lady I need to register with a new doctor there."

I glanced at Kate, whose look gave nothing away. I turned to Miss Mori and her chubby little boy, and reassured her I was not the least offended and was very happy for them. I wished them both luck in their new home and headed swiftly back to the sanctuary of my office.

My mind toyed briefly with the image of Miss Mori arriving for her first consultation with her new GP, requesting with a serious face that she needed a letter to ask for help in moving her furniture to her new house, saying she had heard about the patient transport system which, of course, was free on the poor old NHS.

* By the way, the name Morioriojurereoluwagba translates as 'I have found God's favour'.

THE END

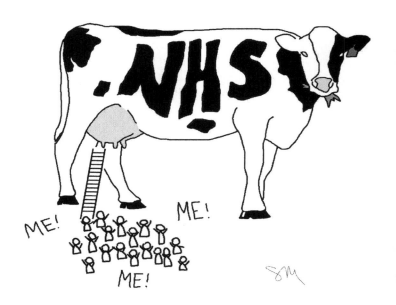

16506886R00055

Printed in Great Britain
by Amazon